COMPLETE POEMS

Wilfred Owen

With an Introduction by Siegfried Sassoon
And a Memoir by Edmund Blunden

Blackthorn Press, Blackthorn House
Middleton Rd, Pickering YO18 8AL
United Kingdom

www.blackthornpress.com

ISBN 978 1 906259 37 2

Cover design by Anthony Avery

Printed and bound by CPI Group (UK) Ltd, Croydon, CR0 4YY

Wilfred Edward Salter Owen 1893 - 1918

CONTENTS

Other Poems and Fragments

Minor Poems and Juvenilia

Index of First Lines

vii

INTRODUCTION

In writing an Introduction such as this it is good to be brief. The poems printed in this book need no preliminary commendations from me or anyone else. The author has left us his own fragmentary but impressive Foreword; this, and his Poems, can speak for him, backed by the authority of his experience as an infantry soldier, and sustained by nobility and originality of style. All that was strongest in Wilfred Owen survives in his poems; any superficial impressions of his personality, any records of his conversation, behaviour, or appearance, would be irrelevant and unseemly. The curiosity which demands such morsels would be incapable of appreciating the richness of his work.

The discussion of his experiments in assonance and dissonance (of which 'Strange Meeting' is the finest example) may be left to the professional critics of verse, the majority of whom will be more preoccupied with such technical details than with the profound humanity of the self-revelation manifested in such magnificent lines as those at the end of his 'Apologia pro Poemate Meo', and in that other poem which he named 'Greater Love'.

The importance of his contribution to the literature of the War cannot be decided by those who, like myself, both admired him as a poet and valued him as a friend. His conclusions about War are so entirely in accordance with my own that I cannot attempt to judge his work with any critical detachment. I can only affirm that he was a man of absolute integrity of mind. He never wrote his poems (as so many war-poets did) to make the effect of a personal gesture. He pitied others; he did not pity himself. In the last year of his life he attained a clear vision of what he needed to say, and these poems survive him as his true and splendid testament

Wilfred Owen was born at Oswestry on 18th March 1893. He was educated at the Birkenhead Institute, and matriculated at London University in 1910. In 1913 he obtained a private tutorship near Bordeaux, where he remained until 1915. During this period he became acquainted with the eminent French poet, Laurent Tailhade, to whom he showed his early verses, and from whom he received considerable encouragement. In 1915, in spite of delicate health, he joined the Artists' Rifles O.T.C., was gazetted to the Manchester Regiment, and served with their 2nd Battalion in France from December 1916 to June 1917, when he was invalided home. Fourteen months later he returned to the Western Front and served with the same Battalion, ultimately commanding a Company.

He was awarded the Military Cross for gallantry while taking part in some heavy fighting on 1st October. He was killed on 4th November 1918, while endeavouring to get his men across the Sambre Canal.

A month before his death he wrote to his mother: "My nerves are in perfect order. I came out again in order to help these boys; directly, by leading them as well as an officer can; indirectly, by watching their sufferings that I may speak of them as well as a pleader can." Let his own words be his epitaph:

> "Courage was mine, and I had mystery;
> Wisdom was mine, and I had mastery."

Siegfried Sassoon.

MEMOIR BY EDMUND BLUNDEN

Twelve years of uneasy peace have passed since the War, among its final victims, took Wilfred Owen, and ten since the choice edition of his poems by his friend Siegfried Sassoon revealed to lovers of poetry and the humanities how great a glory had departed. It is impossible to become deeply acquainted with Owen's work and not to be haunted by comparisons between his genius and his premature death and the wonder and tragedy of his admired Keats. The sense of his promise and achievement has deepened since 1920, and his former editor has been conspicuous among those who have urged the preparation of a new and enlarged volume of Owen's poems, with such biographical notice as can and should be prefixed to them. The reader, who has in his hands a collection of poems by Owen more than twice as extensive as the previous one, will share the present editor's feelings of gratitude to Mrs. Owen and to Mr. Sassoon, who have made the volume possible by the careful preservation and liberal communication of the manuscripts, and whatever documents provided the substance of the memoir. Mrs. Owen, in sending a store of Owen's early notebooks and loose papers for this book, mentions an episode not unfamiliar in the lives of true poets, yet occasioning some natural tears to the devotee of this poet: "He gave me a sack full to burn once, with strict orders 'not to reserve a sheet'. I of course did as he wished—tho' it was like burning my heart."

There survives, however, a quantity of manuscript by Owen, which he had no leisure to organize. Much of it represents the early period of his enthusiasm for poetry, when he was finding his own way to the secrets of style, and discovering the forms of verse on which he would build up his own House Beautiful. These papers are chiefly remarkable as picturing the isolation in which a poet discerns that he is a poet, the delight and difficulty of the high calling to which he finds himself born, and the fruitful uses of practice in thought and its richest verbal presentation. In them, the young Owen is, without knowing it, the guarantor of the eventual poet who, plunged into the abysses of the breaking of nations, has skill to speak. Their fancies, devices, luxuries, concords enabled him to meet the shocks and amazements of immense suffering with the courage of a masterly artist. But I digress too soon and too widely. Early and late, Owen was a productive poet, and that fact, coupled with the fate that denied him opportunity to decide his own poetry, makes the task of editing his manuscripts complicated. Ideas, images, and musical hints rose up in his mind so fast that many of his poems exist in several versions, of which the ultimate 'fair copy' is not to be certainly separated. In reconsidering this problem, and in offering the reader the text and notes before him, I must pay my tribute to the earlier care and insight of Mr. Sassoon, who, it will be remembered, expressed his indebtedness in the preparation of his edition to Miss Edith Sitwell.

Wilfred Owen was born at Plas Wilmot, Oswestry, on March 18, 1893. Another town in which Owen's name is honoured, while the details of his association are scanty, is Birkenhead; and there we know at least the association that he was educated at the Birkenhead Institute. Perhaps, to us who bless him for his poetry, the epoch-making event of his boyhood was a visit to Broxton by the Hill. "Wilfred", his mother informs me, "must have been about ten years old when I took him for a holiday to Broxton"; and a passage that he wrote about ten years after that tells us the rest,

> For I fared back into my life's arrears
> Even the weeks at Broxton, by the Hill,
> Where first I felt my boyhood fill
> With uncontainable movements; there was born
> My poethood.

Some additional words on his childhood from his mother will be welcomed: "He was always a very thoughtful, imaginative child—not very robust, and never cared for games. As a little child his greatest pleasure was for me to read to him even after he could read himself."

When he was thirteen or fourteen, he showed clearly the fascination that poetry had for him. He was also a passionate acquirer of learning. His choice of acquaintance through life depended on the soundness and value of what he could learn from those he met; as Bacon puts it, "a full man" pleased him. His father twice took him to Brittany between his fourteenth year and his sixteenth; there he seized every chance of conversation with French people, and was discontented only when the time came to return home. He could not have guessed that he should live to cry out, "I shall never again beg father to take me to France!"

In 1911 he matriculated at the London University (he had been a day-student for a short time at University College, Reading, where he attended Botany lectures). By that time he had become (with great diffidence, in fear and trembling almost) a writer of verses, and was deep in the work of Keats and others, but particularly Keats. His own verses of such an early date supply an engaging record of that dominant devotion. Their intrinsic merits are not my object in quoting them. A sonnet, entitled 'Written in a Wood, September 1910', stands thus:

> Full ninety autumns hath this ancient beech
> Helped with its myriad leafy tongues to swell
> The dirges of the deep-toned western gale,
> And ninety times hath all its power of speech
> Been stricken dumb, at sound of winter's yell,
> Since Adonais, no more strong and hale,

Might have rejoiced to linger here and teach
His thoughts in sonnets to the listening dell;
Or glide in fancy through those leafy grots
And bird-pavilions hung with arras green,
To hear the sonnets of its minstrel choir.
Ah, ninety times again, when autumn rots,
Shall birds and leaves be mute and all unseen,
{Yet shall Keats' voice sing on and never tire.
{Yet shall I see fair Keats, and hear his lyre.

Another sonnet, dated April 21, 1911, was "written at Teignmouth, on a Pilgrimage to Keats's House"; and in it, with imaginative distinction, the young pilgrim speaks his contentment in a day when the sea seemed to share his proud grief for one "whose name was writ on water". In the summer of 1912, Owen followed Keats in a twofold way by writing a poem 'On Seeing a Lock of Keats's Hair', of which this is the final stanza:

It is a lock of Adonais' hair!
I dare not look too long; nor try to tell
What glories I see glistening, glistening there.
The unanointed eye cannot perceive their spell.
Turn ye to Adonais; his great spirit seek.
     O hear him; he will speak!

But this innocent idolatry did not exclude other influences. One warm day in December 1911 he wrote a letter in verse, from somewhere in Oxfordshire.

Full springs of Thought around me rise
Like Rivers Four to water my fair garden.
Eastwards, where lie wide woodlands, rich as Arden,
From out the beechen solitudes hath sprung
A stream of verse from aerial Shelley's tongue,
While, as he drifted on between the banks
Of happy Thames, the waters 'neath the planks
Of his light boat gurgled contentedly
And ever with his dreams kept company.
To-day, the music of the slow, turmoiling river,
The music of the rapid vision-giver,
To me are vocal both.
                    To eastward, too,
A churchyard sleeps, and one infirm old yew,
Where in the shadows of the fading day,

Musing on faded lives, sate solemn Gray.
There to majestic utterance his soul was wrought,
And still his mighty chant is fraught
With golden teaching for the world, and speaks
Strong things with sweetness unto whoso seeks.
Yet can I never sit low at his feet
And, questioning, a gracious answer meet.
For he is gone, and his high dignity
Lost in the past (tho' he may haply be
Far in Futurity as well).
                    To North
Are hills where Arnold wandered forth
Which, like his verse, still undulate in calm
And tempered beauty.
                    And the marriage-psalm
Was sung o'er Tennyson, small space away.

This rhyming letter has something still more intimate, for, towards its close, Owen declares his longing for a new great poet—for all of us, and himself:

Let me attain
To talk with him, and share his confidence.

His loneliness as a young poet breaks out; he may read even Keats and "still", he appeals, "I am alone among the Unseen Voices".

A serious illness, in 1913, led to his "proceeding to France", as he would have described it a year or two later, with the object of escaping the English winter in its more usual manifestations. He became a tutor at Bordeaux, and remained there long enough to acquire a great deal of the French language—the French way of thinking. At Bordeaux he had the good fortune to become acquainted with that old hero, M. Laurent Tailhade, the poet, well qualified to spur him on in the delicate yet highly original studies of the poetic art which he was making. M. Tailbade wrote, on April 1, 1915: "Votre lettre est charmante. Cette impuissance de vous 'exprimer en francais' qui vous fait hésiter, n'existe que dans votre imagination. Vous peignez avec un délicat pinceau; votre piano a les touches nécessaires pour la grâce et l'émotion." Owen was never troubled with doubts whether a poet should be a curious designer of verses or not; he frankly enjoyed the art of verse. He intended, in 1913, to publish 'Minor Poems—in Minor Keys—By a Minor'. Among those, however, I find one of which the power is so full and the tone so deep and final that Mr. Sassoon, happening upon it in a copy without evidence of date, marks it "Late?" But the poems of the same period are for the most part tentative and without a complete impulse, notwithstanding that some of them are on an ambitious scale. There is an ode on 'The Swift', another on 'Uriconium', and a lengthy tale of the kind that Keats achieved in 'Isabella'— but not from Boccaccio. It is 'The Little Mermaid of Hans Christian Andersen, done into English verse', and extends to seventy-eight stanzas. One of the obvious things about these immature poems is the sensuousness which Owen had in scarcely less degree than even Keats, and the following lines will show it, alike in its command of the unpleasing and the agreeable.

> A tinge
> Curdled the sea, like mingling oil and ink. . . .

> The witch's den! Around was filthy quag,
> In whose soft mire slow-wallowed water-slugs,
> Large, fat and white. There sat the fishy hag,
> Beneath her hut of bones. .

Of golden hair,

> This is more like the aureoles of Aurora,
> The leaves of flames, the flame of her corona.
> Not Petrarch wore such coronals, nor Laura,
> Nor yet his orange-trees by old Verona,
> Nor gay gold fruits that yellow Barcelona!

In the possibilities of splendid colours, in the glories of gems and in music of all kinds his spirit expanded. But as yet the perception of life's values which was to be his was lacking to his poetical passion.

Speculating on his future, he expressed his conclusions in May 1914: "I certainly believe I could make a better musician than many who profess to be, and are accepted as such. Mark, I do not for a moment call myself a musician, nor do I suspect I ever shall be, but there! I love Music, with such *strength* that I have had to conceal the passion, for fear it be thought weakness. . . . Failing Music, is it Pictures that I hanker to do? I am not abashed to admit it, but heigh ho! If there were anything in me I should, following Legend, have covered, with spirited fresco, the shed, or carved the staircase knob into a serene Apollo! . . . Let me now seriously and shamelessly work out a Poem."

In July 1914 Owen, like most of his contemporaries, was intent upon the brighter side of experience, and that month he wrote the ingenious and fresh verses beginning

> Leaves
> Murmuring by myriads in the shimmering trees.
> Lives

> *Wakening with wonder in the Pyrenees.*
>
> Birds
> *Cheerily chirping in the early day.*
>
> Bards
> *Singing of summer scything thro' the hay.*

That note was soon to be changed, and the 'Endymion' phase of Owen's poetical life was at a close. Thenceforward he moved into the sphere of the later 'Hyperion', to the lofty sorrow and threnody of which the latest of his writings must be likened; moreover, when he was to be moved by lighter forces of life, they were to be those of a ghost-like secrecy and dimness. In understanding and expressing those mysterious backwaters of a European war's great current, Owen had the advantage of being attuned to the sadness of the French poets; he is, at moments, an English Verlaine. It did not take him long, after the sudden dismissal of peace, to feel and utter the solemn death of a period, and in himself the transition from a youth of maying to an agedness of mood.

> *Thou hast led me like a heathen sacrifice*
> *With music and with fatal yokes of flowers—*

But he did not display any immediate conception that war was disenchantment, obscenity, and torture. He stood, watching the storm working up, and contemplating the change of empires. He had matured, and was now come to his intellectual stature. He viewed the past, and discerned inevitability. (See the poem 1914).

In 1915—the date of his enlistment was controlled by his tutorial engagement—he returned to England. He joined the Artists' Rifles. His view of the soldier as the victim began to appear in his verses; he had already written a paradoxical 'Ballad of Purchase Moneys', opening with the aspect of new crusades and modern knightliness, closing with the burden of war.

> *The Sun is sweet on rose and wheat*
> *   And on the eyes of children;*
> *Quiet the street for old men's feet*
> *   And gardens for the children.*
>
> *The soil is safe, for widow and waif,*
> *   And for the soul of England,*
> *Because their bodies men vouchsafe*
> *   To save the soul of England.*
>
> *Fair days are yet left for the old,*
> *   And children's cheeks are ruddy,*

Because the good lads' limbs lie cold
And their brave cheeks are bloody.

This was the general position; but Owen, like many others in that multitude of unselfish youth, still had moods in which he regarded his individual life as though no devastating force had arrived to baffle its progress. In a long, self-questioning letter of March 5, 1915, he declared his ambitions as those of a poet: "lesser than Macbeth's and greater, not so happy but much happier". Perhaps, as we all did, he clung to the notion that the War would soon be over. *"To be able* to write as *I know how to,* study is necessary: a period of study, then of intercourse with kindred spirits, then of isolation. My heart is ready, but my brain unprepared, and my hand untrained. I quite envisage possibility of non-success."

Gazetted to the Manchester Regiment, Owen joined the 2nd Battalion in January 1917 on the Somme battlefield, where the last sharp fighting was in progress, in that hardest of winters, before the Germans withdrew to their new trench system. Letters home disclose something of his individual experience and of the general life—now so remote in its singularities—of British infantrymen in Flanders. Before leaving the Base Wilfred wrote: "I have just received Orders to take the train at Étaples, to join the 2nd Manchesters. This is a Regular Regiment, so I have come off mighty well. . . .It is a huge satisfaction to be going among well-trained troops and genuine 'real-old' officers. . . . This morning I was hit! We were bombing, and a fragment from somewhere hit my thumb knuckle. I coaxed out one drop of blood. Alas! no more!! There is a fine heroic feeling about being in France, and I am in perfect spirits. A tinge of excitement is about me, but excitement is always necessary to my happiness." On January 4, he wrote a fuller review of the process which took place between a training-camp and a company in the Line: "I have joined the Regiment, who are just at the end of a six weeks' rest. I will not describe the awful vicissitudes of the journey here. I arrived at Folkestone, and put up at the best hotel. It was a place of luxury—inconceivable now— carpets as deep as the mud here—golden flunkeys; pages who must have been melted into their clothes and expanded since; even the porters had clean hands. Even the dogs that licked up the crumbs had clean teeth. Since I set foot on Calais quays I have not had dry feet. No one knew anything about us on this side, and we might have taken weeks to get here, and *must* have, but for fighting our way here. At the Base, as I said, it was not so bad. We were in the camp of Sir Percy Cunynghame, who had bagged for his Mess the Duke of Connaught's chef. After those two days, we were let down, gently, into the real thing, mud. It has penetrated now into that sanctuary, my sleeping bag, and that holy of holies, my pyjamas. For I sleep on a stone floor, and the servant squashed mud on all my belongings; I suppose by way of baptism. We are 3 officers in this 'Room', the rest of the house is occupied by servants and the band; the roughest set of knaves I have ever been herded with.

Even now their language is shaking the flimsy door between the rooms. I chose a servant for myself yesterday, not for his profile, nor yet for clean hands, but for his excellence in bayonet work. For the servant is always at the side of his officer in the charge, and is therefore worth a dozen nurses. Alas, he of the Bayonet is in the Bombing Section, and it is against Regulations to employ such as a servant. I makeshift with another. Everything is makeshift. The English seem to have fallen into the French unhappy-go-lucky non-system. There are scarcely any houses here. The men lie in barns. Our Mess Room is also an Ante and Orderly Room. We eat and drink out of old tins, some of which show traces of ancient enamel. We are never dry, and never 'off duty'. On all the officers' faces there is a harassed look that I have never seen before, and which in England never will be seen—out of jails. The men are just as Bairnsfather has them—expressionless lumps. We feel the weight of them hanging on us. I have found not a few of the old Fleetwood Musketry party here. They seemed glad to see me, as far as the set doggedness of their features would admit. I censored hundreds of letters yesterday, and the hope of peace was in every one. The *Daily Mail* map, which appeared about Jan. 2, will be of extreme interest to you. We were stranded in a certain town one night, and I saved the party of us by collaring an Orderly in the streets and making him take us to a Sergeants' Mess. . . . I am perfectly well and strong, but unthinkably dirty and squalid. I scarcely dare to wash. Pass on as much of this happy news as may interest people. The favourite song of the men is,

> *The Roses round the door*
> *Makes me love mother more.*

They sing this everlastingly. I don't disagree."

    Sunday, Jan. 7, 1917. "It is afternoon. We had an Inspection to make from 9 to 12 this morning. I have wandered into a village café where they gave me writing paper. We made a redoubtable march yesterday from the last Camp to this. The awful state of the roads, and the enormous weight carried, was too much for scores of men. Officers also carried full packs, but I had a horse part of the way. It was beginning to freeze through the rain when we arrived at our tents. We were at the mercy of the cold, and, being in health, I never suffered so terribly as yesterday afternoon. I am really quite well, but have sensations kindred to being seriously ill. As I was making my damp bed, I heard the guns for the first time. It was a sound not without a certain sublimity. They woke me again at 4 o'clock. We are two in a tent. I am with the Lewis Gun Officer. We begged stretchers from the doctor to sleep on. Our servant brings our food to us in our tents. This would not be so bad, but for lack of water and the intense damp cold. . . . This morning I have been reading Trench Standing Orders to my platoon *(verb, sap.)*. Needless to say I show a cheerier face to them than I wear in writing this letter; but I must not disguise from you the fact that we are at one of the worst parts of the Line. . . . I can't tell you any more Facts. I have no Fancies and no Feelings. Positively they went numb with my feet. Love is not quenched, except the unenduring flickerings thereof." Two days later he reports: "We moved further up yesterday, most of the way on 'buses. I have just had your long-looked-for letter. It seems wrong that ever your dear handwriting should come into such a Gehenna as this. There is a terrific strafe on. The artillery are doing a 48 hours' bombardment. At night it is like a stupendous thunderstorm, for the flashes are quite as bright as lightning. When we arrived at this deserted village last night, there had been no billets prepared for the battalion—owing to misunderstanding. Imagine the confusion! For my part I discovered, or rather my new-chosen and faithful servant discovered, a fine little hut, with a chair in it. A four-legged chair! The roof is waterproof, and there is a stove. There is only one slight disadvantage: there is a howitzer just 70 or 80 yards away, firing over the top every minute or so. I can't tell you how glad I am you got me the ear-defenders. I have to wear them at night. Every time No. 2 (the nearest gun) fires, all my pharmacopœia, all my boots, candle, and nerves take a smart jump upwards. This phenomenon is immediately followed by a fine rain of particles from the roof. I keep blowing them off the page. From time to time the village is shelled, but just now nothing is coming over. Anyhow there is a good cellar close to. . . I spent an hour to-day behind the guns (to get used to them). The major commanding the battery was very pleasant indeed. He took me to his H.Q., and gave me a book of poems to read as if it were the natural thing to do!! But all night I shall be hearing the fellow's voice:

'Number TWO—FIRE!'"

That same afternoon, his next letter mentions, he "took a tour into the Line which we shall occupy. Our little party was shelled going up across the open country. It was not at all frightful, and only one 4.7 got anywhere near, falling plump in the road, but quite a minute after we had passed the spot. I tell you these things because *afterwards* they will sound less exciting. . . . My Company Commander (A Company) has been out here since the beginning: 'tis a gentleman *and an original* (!) Next in command is Haydon, whom I greatly like. . . . Even as they prophesied in the Artists, I have to take a close interest in feet, and this very day I knelt down with a candle and watched each man perform his anointment with whale oil; praising the clean feet, but not reviling the unclean. . . . I am not allowed to send a sketch, but you must know I am transformed now, wearing a steel helmet, buff-jerkin of leather, rubber-waders up to the hips, and gauntlets. But for the rifle, we are exactly like Cromwellian Troopers. The waders are indispensable. In 2½ miles of trench which I waded yesterday there was not one inch of dry ground. There is a mean depth of 2 feet of water. . . . These things I need: (1) small pair nail scissors; (2) celluloid hair-pin box from Boots' with *tight-fitting lid,* and containing boracic powder; (3)

Player's 'Navy Cut'; (4) ink pellets; (5) Sweets (!!). We shall not be in touch with supplies by day."

This heralded his first trench tour, on the St. Quentin front. On January 16 he wrote: "I can see no excuse for deceiving you about these last 4 days. I have suffered seventh hell. I have not been at the front. I have been in front of it. I held an advanced post, that is, a 'dug-out' in the middle of No Man's Land. We had a march of 3 miles over shelled road, then nearly 3 along a flooded trench. After that we came to where the trenches had been blown flat out and had to go over the top. It was of course dark, too dark, and the ground was not mud, not sloppy mud, but an octopus of sucking clay, 3, 4, and 5 feet deep, relieved only by craters full of water. Men have been known to drown in them. Many stuck in the mud and only got on by leaving their waders, equipment, and in some cases their clothes. High explosives were dropping all around, and machine-guns spluttered every few minutes. But it was so dark that even the German flares did not reveal us. Three-quarters dead, I mean each of us ¾ dead, we reached the dug-out and relieved the wretches therein. I then had to go forth and find another dug-out for a still more advanced post where I left 18 bombers. I was responsible for other posts on the left, but there was a junior officer in charge. My dug-out held 25 men tight packed. Water filled it to a depth of 1 or 2 feet, leaving say 4 feet of air. One entrance had been blown in and blocked. So far, the other remained. The Germans knew we were staying there and decided we shouldn't. Those fifty hours were the agony of my happy life. Every ten minutes on Sunday afternoon seemed an hour. I nearly broke down and let myself drown in the water that was now slowly rising over my knees. Towards 6 o'clock, when, I suppose, you would be going to church, the shelling grew less intense and less accurate; so that I was mercifully helped to do my duty and crawl, wade, climb, and flounder over No Man's Land to visit my other post. It took me half an hour to move about 150 yards. I was chiefly annoyed by our own machine-guns from behind. The seeng-seeng-seeng of the bullets reminded me of Mary' canary. On the whole I can support the canary better. In the platoon on my left the sentries over the dug-out were blown to nothing. One of these poor fellows was my first servant whom I rejected. If I had kept him he would have lived, for servants don't do sentry duty. I kept my own sentries half-way down the stairs during the more terrific bombardment. In spite of this one lad was blown down and, I am afraid, blinded. This was my only casualty. The officer of the left platoon has come out completely prostrated and is in hospital. I am now as well, I suppose, as ever. I allow myself to tell you all these things because *I am never going back to this awful post.* It is the worst the Manchesters have ever held; and we are going back for a rest. I hear that the officer who relieved me left his 3 Lewis guns behind when he came out. (He had only 24 hours in). He will be court-martialled."

Rest, with the infantry on the Western Front, became a term of irony. January 19, 1917: "We are now a long way back, in a ruined village, all huddled together in a farm. We all sleep in the same room where we eat and try to live. My bed is a hammock of rabbit-wire stuck up beside a great shell-hole in the wall. Snow is deep about, and melts through the gaping roof, on to my blanket. We are wretched beyond my previous imagination—but safe. Last night indeed I had to 'go up' with a party. We got lost in the snow. I went on ahead to scout—foolishly alone—and, when half a mile away from the party, got overtaken by

GAS.

It was only tear-gas from a shell, and I got safely back (to the party) in my helmet, with nothing worse than a severe fright! And a few tears, some natural, some unnatural. . . .Coal, water, candles, accommodation, everything is scarce. We have not always air! When I took my helmet off last night—O Air, it was a heavenly thing! . . . They want to call No Man's Land 'England' because we keep supremacy there. It is like the eternal place of gnashing of teeth; the Slough of Despond could be contained in one of its crater-holes; the fires of Sodom and Gomorrah could not light a candle to it—to find the way to Babylon the Fallen. It is pock-marked like a body of foulest disease, and its odour is the breath of cancer. I have not seen any dead. I have done worse. In the dank air I have *perceived* it, and in the darkness, *felt.* Those 'Somme Pictures' are the laughing-stock of the army—like the trenches on exhibition in Kensington. No Man's Land under snow is like the face of the moon, chaotic, crater-ridden, uninhabitable, awful, the abode of madness. To call it 'England'! I would as soon call my House (!) Krupp Villa, or my child Chlorina-Phosgena. . . . The people of England needn't hope. They must agitate. But they are not yet agitated even. Let them imagine 50 strong men trembling as with ague for 50 hours!"

The winter of 1916—1917 will long be remembered for its scarcely tolerable cold. The 2nd Manchesters did not get the rest expected, and Owen was soon in the front line again. "In this place my platoon had no dug-outs, but had to lie in the snow under the deadly wind. By day it was impossible to stand up, or even crawl about, because we were behind only a little ridge screening us from the Boche's periscope. We had 5 Tommy's Cookers between the platoon, but they did not suffice to melt the ice in the water-cans. So we suffered cruelly from thirst. The marvel is that we did not all die of cold. As a matter of fact, only one of my party actually froze to death before he could be got back, but I am not able to tell how many have ended in hospital. I had no real casualties from shelling, though for 10 minutes every hour whizz-bangs fell a few yards short of us. Showers of soil rained on us but no fragment of shell could find us. . . . My feet ached until they could ache no more, and so they temporarily died. I was kept warm by the ardour of Life within me. I forgot hunger in the hunger for Life. . . . I cannot say I felt any fear. We were all half-crazed by the buffeting of the high explosives. I think the most unpleasant reflection that weighed on me was the impossibility of getting back any wounded, a total impossibility by day, and frightfully difficult by night. We were marooned on a frozen desert. There is not a sign of life on the horizon, and a thousand signs of death. Not a blade of grass, not an insect; once or twice a day the shadow of a big hawk, scenting carrion. By degrees, day by day, we worked back through the reserve and support lines to the crazy village where the Battalion takes breath. While in support we inhabited vast Boche dug-outs (full of all kinds of souvenirs). They are so deep that they seem warm like mines! There we began to thaw. . . . Then I had the heavenly-dictated order to proceed on a Transport Course. Me in Transports? Aren't you ?" He was writing from the riding school at Amiens, on February 4, with the prospect of a month's exercise (he was a natural horseman) and lodgings "in a HOUSE". "Quite 10 years ago I made a study of this town and cathedral, in the Treasury. It is all familiar now!" He looked at the "inoffensive sky" and his room, and reflected, "I suppose I can endure cold and fatigue and the face-to-face death as well as another; but extra for me there is the universal pervasion of *Ugliness.* Hideous landscapes, vile noises, foul language, and nothing but foul, even from one's own mouth (for all are devil-ridden)—everything unnatural, broken, blasted; the distortion of the dead, whose unburiable bodies sit outside the dug-outs all day, all night, the most execrable sights on earth. In poetry we call them the most glorious. But to sit with them all day, all night—and a week later to come back and find them still sitting there in motionless groups, THAT is what saps the 'soldierly spirit'."

On March 1 he rejoined his battalion in the extreme south of the British trench line, recently taken over from the French. It was quiet—"so quiet that we have our meals in a shallow dug-out, and only go down deep to sleep". He was soon kept busy in charge of digging parties. On March 14 he reported an accident at Le Quesnoy-en-Santerre of a kind which might easily have been more frequent in the devastated area: "Last night I was going round through pitch darkness to see a man in a dangerous state of exhaustion. I fell into a kind of well, only about 15 ft., but I caught the back of my head on the way down. The doctors (not in consultation!) say I have a slight concussion. Of course I have a vile headache, but I don't feel at all fuddled." Five days later he wrote again of this mishap. "I am in a hospital bed (for the first time in life). After falling into that hole (which I believe was a shell-hole in a floor, laying open a deep cellar) I felt nothing more than a headache, for 3 days; and went up to the front in the usual way—or nearly the usual way, for I felt too weak to wrestle with the mud, and sneaked along the top, snapping my fingers at a clumsy sniper. When I got back I developed a high fever, vomited strenuously and long, and was seized with muscular pains. The night before last I was sent to a shanty a bit farther back, and yesterday motored on to this Field Hospital, called Casualty Clearing Station 13." He added that he felt better, and, on March 21, that he was getting up and expecting soon "to overtake my Battalion" again. However, it was in hospital that he drafted (March 23) the sonnet "With an Identity Disc".

The battalion had been attacking, and he 'caravanned' to them over unfamiliar territory. On the way he had one night's lodging "with a family of refugees, 3 boys, 2 tiny girls: a good class socially, and of great charm personally. I was treated as a god, and indeed begin to suspect I have a heart as comprehensive as Victor Hugo's, Shakespeare's, or your own." (He is writing to his mother.) "In 24 hours I never took so many hugs and kisses in my life, no, not in the first chapter even. They took reliefs at it. It would have astounded the English mind." He found his battalion, and was very welcome, for they had not made their successful attack without heavy losses. Then—"We stuck to our line 4 days (and 4 nights) without relief, in the open, and in the snow. Not an hour passed without a shell amongst us. I never went off to sleep on those days, because the others were far more fagged after several days of fighting than I fresh from bed. We lay in wet snow. I kept alive on brandy, the fear of death, and the glorious prospect of the cathedral town just below us, glittering with the morning. With glasses I could easily make out the general architecture of the cathedral: so I have told you how near we have got. The French are on the skirts of the town, as I could see. It was unknown where exactly the Boche was lying in front of us. The job of finding out fell upon me. I started out at midnight with 2 corporals and 6 picked men, warning other regiments on our flanks not to make any mistake about us. It was not very long before the Hun sent up his Very lights, but the ground was favourable to us, and I and my corporal prowled on until we clearly heard voices, and the noises of carrying and digging. When I had seen them quite clearly moving about, and marked the line of their entrenchment, it might seem my job was done; but my orders were to discover the force of the enemy. So then I took an inch or two of cover and made a noise like a platoon. Instantly we had at least two machine-guns turned on us, and a few odd rifles. Then we made a scramble for 'home'. Another night I was putting out an advanced post when we were seen or heard and greeted with shrapnel. The man crouching shoulder to shoulder to me gets a beautiful round hole pierced deep in his biceps. I am nothing so fortunate, being only buffeted in the eyes by the shock and whacked on the calf by a spent fragment, which scarcely tore the puttee."

Almost three weeks passed before his next letter (April 25). He had been in attack in the period. "Never before has the Battalion encountered such intense shelling as rained upon us as we advanced in the open. . . . The reward we got for all this was to remain in the Line 12 days. For twelve days I did not wash my face, nor take off my boots, nor sleep a deep sleep. For twelve days we lay in holes, where at any moment a shell might put us out. I think the worst incident was one wet night when we lay up against a railway embankment. A big shell lit on the top of the bank, just 2 yards from my head. Before I awoke, I was blown in the air right away from the bank! I passed most of the following days in a railway cutting, in a hole just big enough to lie in, and covered with corrugated iron. My brother officer of B Coy., 2nd Lt. G., lay opposite in a similar hole. But he was covered with earth, and no relief will ever relieve him, nor will his Rest be a 9-days—Rest." From this railway cutting it was Owen's duty "about midnight to flounder across to the French and knock at the door of the Company H. Q. and ask if all was well, to be answered by a grunt".

"I think that the terribly long time we stayed unrelieved was unavoidable; yet it makes us feel bitterly towards those in England who might relieve us, and will not. We are now doing what is called a Rest, but we rise at 6.15 and work without break until about 10 P.M., for there is always a Pow-Wow for officers after dinner. And if I have not written yesterday, it is because I must have kept hundreds of letters uncensored, and inquiries about missing men unanswered." Part of this letter is written on a military document. "I hope", says Owen, "this bit of paper is not incriminating to send over." The document, which recalls the Western Front in a decidedly unpopular aspect, reads:

AMENDMENT
S.S. 143—"INSTRUCTIONS FOR THE TRAINING OF
PLATOONS FOR OFFENSIVE ACTION, 1917."

Appendix 1.—NOTES—LINE 6. *After* "No. 1" *add*
"and No. 2".

On May 2 he wrote from the 13th Casualty Clearing Station: "Here again! The Doctor suddenly was moved to forbid me to go into action next time the Battalion go, which will be in a day or two. I did not go sick or anything, but he is nervous about my nerves, and sent me down yesterday—labelled Neurasthenia. I still of course suffer from the headaches traceable to my concussion. . . . Do not for a moment suppose I have had a 'breakdown'! I am simply avoiding one." Joking over his having escaped actual wounds, he remembers, "I should certainly have got a bullet wound, if I had not used the utmost caution in wriggling along the ground on one occasion. There was a party of Germans in a wood about 200 yards *behind* us, and his trench, which we had just taken, was only a foot deep in places, and I was obliged to keep passing up and down it. As a matter of fact I rather enjoyed the evening after the stunt, being only a few hundred yards from the town, as you knew, and having come through the fire so miraculously, and being, moreover, well fed on the Boche's untouched repast!! It was curious and troubling to pick up his letters where he had left off writing in the middle of a word!"

Owen also sent an account of this attack to a brother who might have illusions of the romance of war (May 14). "The sensations of going over the top are about as exhilarating as those dreams of falling over a precipice, when you see the rocks at the bottom surging up to you. I woke up without being squashed. Some didn't. There was an extraordinary exultation in the act of slowly walking forward, showing ourselves openly. There was no bugle and no drum, for which

I was very sorry. I kept up a kind of chanting sing-song:

Keep the Line straight!
Not so fast on the left!
Steady on the left!
Not so fast!

Then we were caught in a tornado of shells. The various 'waves' were all broken up, and we carried on like a crowd moving off a cricket-field. When I looked back and saw the ground all crawling and wormy with wounded bodies, I felt no horror at all, but only an immense exultation at having got through the barrage. We were more than an hour moving over the open, and by the time we came to the German trench every Boche had fled. But a party of them had remained, lying low in a wood close behind us, and they gave us a very bad time for the next four hours. When we were marching along a sunken road, we got the wind up once. We knew we must have passed the German out-posts somewhere on our left rear. All at once the cry rang down, 'Line the bank'. There was a tremendous scurry of fixing bayonets, tugging of breech-covers, and opening pouches, but when we peeped over, behold a solitary German, haring along towards us, with his head down and his arms stretched in front of him, as if he were going to take a high dive through the earth (which I have no doubt he would like to have done). Nobody offered to shoot him, he looked too funny; and that was our only prisoner that day!"

Passing a sunny idleness in scenery which reminded him of the Faerie Queene and of Arthur in Avalon, he nevertheless found himself with a high temperature, and believed he had trench fever. He remained in the Casualty Clearing Station until June 6, when he wrote: "I go down to-day. Where to? Nobody knows. Maybe in the Hospital Train for days."

About June 10, after confused arrangements, Owen was at No. 1 General Hospital. "I think it is very likely that the Americans will send me to England." And a week later he was at the Welsh Hospital, Netley, "in too *receptive* a mood to speak at all about the other side, the seamy side of the 'Manche'. I just wander about absorbing Hampshire."

One of Owen's letters from the hospital on the Somme may be conveniently quoted at this point. It sums up the creed which had taken bold form in his mind, and awaited poetical completion: "Already I have comprehended a light which never will filter into the dogma of any national church: namely, that one of Christ's essential commands was: Passivity at any price! Suffer dishonour and disgrace, but never resort to arms. Be bullied, be outraged, be killed; but do not kill. It may be a chimerical and an ignominious principle, but there it is. It can only be ignored; and I think pulpit professionals are ignoring it very skilfully and successfully indeed. . . . And am I not myself a conscientious objector with a very seared conscience? . . . Christ is literally in 'no man's land'. There men often hear His voice: Greater love hath no man than this, that a man lay down his life for a friend. Is it spoken in English only and French? I do not believe so. Thus you see how pure Christianity will not fit in with pure patriotism."

From Netley, he was sent to what he described on June 26 as "a decayed hydro"—the Craiglockhart War Hospital, a short way out of Edinburgh. "At present", he wrote on August 8, clearly feeling the War's influence even more deeply than before, "I am a sick man in hospital, by night; a poet for quarter of an hour after breakfast; I am whatever and whoever I see while going down to Edinburgh on the train: greengrocer, policeman, shopping lady, errand-boy, paper-boy, blind man, crippled Tommy, bank-clerk, carter, all of these in half an hour; next a German student in earnest; then I either peer over bookstalls, in back-streets, or do a bit of a dash down Princes Street—according as I have taken weak tea or strong coffee for breakfast. . . . Yes, you will like to read Mrs. Browning. Having listened so long to her low, sighing voice (which *can* be *heard* often through the page), and having seen her hair, not in a museum case, but palpably in visions, and having received kindness from a boy to whom she was kind (M. Léger—he is still a boy); for these reasons, I say, the Flapper flaps in vain. The other day I read a biography of Tennyson, which says he was unhappy, even in the midst of his fame, wealth, and domestic serenity. Divine discontent! I can quite believe he never knew happiness for one moment such as I have—for one or two moments. But as for misery, was he ever frozen alive, with dead men for comforters? Did he hear the moaning at the Bar, not at twilight and the evening bell only, but at dawn, noon, and night, eating and sleeping, walking and working, always the close moaning of the Bar; the thunder, the hissing, and the whining of the Bar?—Tennyson, it seems, was always a great child. So should I have been, but for Beaumont Hamel. (Not before January 1917 did I write the *only* lines of mine that carry the stamp of maturity—these:

> *But the old happiness is unreturning,*
> *Boys have no grief as grievous as youth's yearning;*
> *Boys have no sadness sadder than our hope.)*

. . . It is worthy of mention that we have been in mist for 3 days: a gloriously luminous mist at times. I saw Holyrood on Sunday afternoon (being alone on Salisbury Crags), a floating mirage in gold mist; a sight familiar enough in dreams and poems, but which I never thought possible in these islands. It was the picture of a picture. . . ."

At Craiglockhart he was enterprising; he performed at concerts, he lectured, and he edited the hospital magazine called *The Hydra*. About the beginning of August, Captain Siegfried Sassoon arrived. Owen had been reading his *Old Huntsman*. "Nothing like his trench-life sketches has ever been written or ever will be written." One day he ventured to call at his hero's room and to show him some poems, which received some praise and some blame. On the evening of September 7, again, "Sassoon called me in to him; and having condemned some of my poems, amended others, and rejoiced over a few, he read me his very last works, which are superb beyond anything in his book. . . . I don't tell him so, or that I am not worthy to light his pipe. I simply sit tight and tell him where I think he goes wrong." There is a letter of September 22 almost dithyrambic in honour of Mr. Sassoon "as a man, as a friend, and as a poet", and in another Owen refers modestly to "my recent efforts in Sassoon's manner". *The Hydra* was a fortunate periodical; it received new poems by the two best English war-poets. The chance that gave Owen the friendship of Mr. Sassoon, then endeavouring in all ways open to him, but above all by poetical challenge, to shed light on the futile ugliness of the War, was a good one. It supplied the answer to the petition for a poet's companionship which, as has been seen, Owen uttered in his verses years before. To ascribe to it altogether the subsequent self-revelation of Owen as a poet would be in-correct, but the impact of Mr. Sassoon's character, thought, and independent poetic method gave the other a new purpose. Owen might have agreed with the author of *Hudibras*—

> *An English poet should be tried by his peers,*
> *And not by pedants and philosophers,*

—on this occasion. The trial brought out his greatness and directed his passion. With a clear and spacious view of the function of poetry, he rapidly produced the poems which have made him famous.

The problem of dating most of Owen's papers is such that one cannot be sure when he thought out the use of assonances, instead of rhymes, which he perfected. He was, as I have said, an unwearied worker in the laboratory of word, rhythm, and music of language, partly by nature and partly from his close acquaintance with French poetry and its exacting technical subtleties.

Having discovered and practised pararhyme, Owen became aware that it would serve him infinitely in the voicing of emotion and imagination. What he made of it is felt at its fullest, perhaps, in the solemn music of 'Strange Meeting', but again and again by means of it he creates remoteness, darkness, emptiness, shock, echo, the last word. So complete and characteristic is his deployment of this technical resource that imitators have been few; but, indeed, there is another cause why they have been so. Only an innate, unconventional command over language, and a rich and living vocabulary— in short, only a genius for poetry could for long work in that uncommon medium.

The doctor who had charge of Owen at Craiglockhart, A. Brock, took more than common interest in him, regarding him as "a very outstanding figure, both in intellect and in character". In order to restore his nerves to serenity, Dr. Brock directed his energies to any peaceful pursuit that could be arranged; he proposed to him the writing of a poem on a classical subject, 'Antaeus', put him in touch with the Edinburgh 'submerged tenth', and caused him to give lectures at Tynecastle School. At one time Owen was busy with historical research in the Advocates' Library, at the request of Lord Guthrie, whose great courtesy fascinated him. When, towards the end of October, the question of Owen's transference from Craiglockhart arose imminently, he was unhappy: "I am seriously beginning to have aching sensations at being rooted up from this pleasant Region".

I am indebted to Mrs. Mary Gray, who knew Owen well at this period, for an account of his personality. "The bond which drew us together was an intense pity for suffering humanity—a need to alleviate it, wherever possible, and an inability to shirk the sharing of it, even when this seemed useless. This was the keynote of Wilfred's character; indeed it was, simply, Wilfred. His sensitiveness, his sympathy were so acute, so profound, that direct personal experience and individual development can hardly be said to have existed for him. He could only suffer, or rejoice, vicariously. . . .The objection that he overlooked individual emotion could only be urged by small natures, selfishly engrossed in their woes. To anyone else, it was immediately evident that their troubles and their happiness were his. . . . He was naturally silent, but with a silence more expressive than words. He had a wonderful tenderness. Silent and reserved as he was, he was adored by my little girl of eight months old. He was never, at that time, gay or playful, but he had that tenderness and a wonderful smile—a sort of gentle radiance, and the tacit understanding between him and the child was almost uncanny. It was the same with a large family of very poor children, and their parents. I was interested in an Italian one-eyed street singer with a most tragic history and fine personality. His courage, cheerfulness, and philosophy drew Wilfred to him at once. We went often to their very poor, exquisitely kept home in the slums, where again, despite his silence, gentle gravity, and reserve, Wilfred was adored—there is no other word for it. He suffered deeply from diffidence, and self-distrust. This was entirely unconnected with any consideration of the impression he made on others. He set himself immensely high standards, and in moments of despondency grieved deeply over what he regarded, quite unjustifiably, as his failure to live up to them. Nevertheless, in his most despondent moods he could never be said to have experienced despair. His courage was too indomitable for that, and he never laid down his arms. . . .Throughout this trial he kept alight the spark of divine fire—the steadfast belief that through suffering do we attain to the only true spiritual beauty."

After Craiglockhart, Owen went to Scarborough, and at first, by way of light duty, was appointed major-domo of the hotel where the seventy officers of the 5th (Reserve) Battalion, Manchester Regiment, assembled.

The following excerpts from a letter written by him in November 1917, while they disclose the honour in which he held the recipient, Mr. Sassoon, also give a better impression of Owen's spirit at the time than would be otherwise recoverable. "Know that since mid-September, when you still regarded me as a tiresome little knocker on your door, I held you as Keats + Christ + Elijah + my Colonel + my father-confessor + Amenophis IV. in profile. What's that mathematically? . . . If you consider what the above names have severally done for me, you will know what you are doing. And you have *fixed* my Life—however short. You did not light me: I was always a mad comet; but you have fixed me. I spun round you a satellite for a month, but I shall swing out soon, a dark star in the orbit where you will blaze. It is some consolation to know that Jupiter himself sometimes swims out of ken.

"To come back to our sheep, as the French *never* say, I have had a perfect little note from Robert Ross, and have arranged a meeting at 12.30 on Nov. 9th. He mentioned staying at Half-Moon St., but the house is full.

"I have ordered several copies of *Fairies and Fusiliers,* but shall not buy all, in order to leave the book exposed on the Shrewsbury counters! I'm also getting Colvin's new *Life of Keats*—no price advertised, but, damn it, I'm to enjoy my leave! . . .

"What I most miss in Edinburgh (not Craiglockhart) is the conviviality of the Four Boys (L. *vivere—to* live). Some day I must tell how we sang, shouted, whistled, and danced through the dark lanes through Colinton; and how we laughed till the meteors showered round us, and we fell calm under the winter stars. And some of us saw the pathway of the spirits for the first time. And seeing it so far above us, and feeling the good road so safe beneath us, we praised God with louder whistling; and knew we loved one another as no men love for long.

"Which, if the bridge-players, Craig and Lockhart, could have seen, they would have called down the wrath of Jahveh, and buried us under the fires of the City you wot of."

Following an ancient custom of mankind, he reviewed the past on the last day of 1917, writing thus to his mother: "And so I have come to the true measure of man. I am not dissatisfied [with] my years. Everything has been done in bouts: Bouts of awful labour at Shrewsbury and Bordeaux; bouts of amazing pleasure in the Pyrenees, and play at Craiglockhart; bouts of religion at Dunsden; bouts of horrible danger on the Somme; bouts of poetry always; of your affection always; of sympathy for the oppressed always. I go out of this year a poet, my dear mother, as which I did not enter it. I am held peer by the Georgians; I am a poet's poet. I am started. The tugs have left me; I feel the great swelling of the open sea taking my galleon. Last year, at this time (it is just midnight, and now is the intolerable instant of the Change), last year I lay awake in a windy tent in the middle of a vast, dreadful encampment. It seemed neither France nor England, but a kind of paddock where the beasts are kept a few days before the shambles. I heard the revelling of the Scotch troops, who are now dead, and who knew they would be dead. I thought of this present night, and whether I should indeed—whether we should indeed—whether you would indeed—but I thought neither long nor deeply, for I am a master of elision. But chiefly I thought of the very strange look on all faces in that camp; an incomprehensible look, which a man will never see in England, though wars should be in England; nor can it be seen in any battle. But only in Étaples. It was not despair, or terror, it was more terrible than terror, for it was a blindfold look, and without expression, like a dead rabbit's. It will never be painted, and no actor will ever seize it. And to describe it, I think I must go back and be with them. We are sending seven officers straight out to-morrow. I have not said what I am thinking this night, but next December I will surely do so."

The life that was customarily endured in home camps during 1918 had little (other than mere security) to recommend it, particularly to those who remembered the prevailing good-nature and resourceful activity of the armies in Flanders. Owen wrote to his mother in May 1918, of old associations and of his poetry. "I've been busy this evening with my terrific poem (at present) called 'The Deranged'. This poem the Editor of the *Burlington Magazine*—(a 2/6 Arts Journal which takes no poetry)—old More Adey, I say, solemnly prohibited me from sending to the *English Review,* on the grounds that 'the *English Review* should not be encouraged'!!! Five years ago this would, as you suggest, have turned my head—but nowadays my head turns only in shame away from these first flickers of the limelight. For I am old already for a poet, and so little is yet achieved.

"And I want no limelight, and celebrity is the last infirmity I desire.

"Fame is the recognition of one's peers. I have already more than their recognition. . . . Behold, are they not already as many Keatses? As I looked out into the untravelled world over the hedges of Dunsden Garden, I saw them in the dawn and made ready to go out and meet them.

"And they were glad and rejoiced, though I am the gravest and least witty of that grave, witty company."

Among those who had become aware that a new soldier-poet called Owen was arriving, I find the names of Robert Ross, Roderick Meiklejohn, H. W. Massingham, H. G. Wells, Arnold Bennett, and Osbert Sitwell; and Owen was delighted to find himself at last within the circle of men of letters. There was a project of publishing his poems, and William Heinemann, despite "the state of the paper supply", expressed a willingness to undertake it, or at least to consider it. Another author whose acquaintance he made was Charles Scott-Moncrieff, who obtained Owen's criticism and advice for his translation of the 'Song of Roland'. That work was originally dedicated 'To Mr. W. O.', with a tribute to his mastery of the art of poetry; when it was published in 1919, it contained instead a group of poems in memory of three friends, one of which is a sonnet to Owen:

In the centuries of time to come
Men shall be happy *and rehearse thy fame.*

Scott-Moncrieff, then at the War Office, endeavoured to find some post for Owen which would mean that he would be kept in England. On May 21, Owen had some prospect "of becoming Instructing Staff Officer to a Cadet Battalion. I would *rather,*" he wrote, "work in the War Office itself, and that seems not impossible either. Really I would *like most* to go to Egypt or Italy, but that is not entertained by Scott-Moncrieff" In the end, none of these plans or wishes materialized.

At the close of July he was preparing to go overseas. "Now must I throw my little candle on [Sassoon's] torch and go out again. There are rumours of a large draft of officers shortly." A few days later he reported that he was to attend for medical inspection, and would proceed to France. "I am glad. That is I am much gladder to be going out again than afraid. I shall be better able to cry my outcry, playing my part. The secondary annoyances and discomforts of France behind the line can be no worse than this Battalion. On Friday we were called up at 3 A.M. and had the usual day's work. The Adjutant is ill, and Stiebel is ill. I did Stiebel's job on the stunt, and am still doing it. There are only mock alarms of course. But this morning at 8.20 we heard a boat torpedoed in the bay, about a mile out, they say who saw it. I think only 10 lives were saved. I wish the Boche would have the pluck to come right in and make a clean sweep of the pleasure boats, and the promenaders on the Spa, and all the stinking Leeds and Bradford war-profiteers now reading *John Bull* on Scarborough Sands."

Other letters carry Owen's story towards its untimely close. There was a last day with his mother. Looking with her across the Channel, he repeated a favourite passage from Rabindranath Tagore: "When I go from hence, let this be my parting word, that what I have seen is unsurpassable". On August 31, 1918, he reported his embarkation to Mr. Sassoon: "I have been incoherent ever since I tried to say good-bye on the steps of Lancaster Gate. But everything is clear now; and I'm in hasty retreat towards the Front. Battle is easier here; and therefore you will stay and endure old men and women to the End, and wage the bitterer war and more hopeless." Another message followed quickly: "The sun is warm, the sky is clear, the waves are dancing fast and bright. But these are not Lines written in Dejection. Serenity Shelley never dreamed of crowns me. Will it last when I shall have gone into Caverns and Abysmals such as he never reserved for his worst daemons? . . . And now I am among the herds again, a Herdsman; and a Shepherd of sheep that do not know my voice." Such was, indeed, the feeling of a young officer with temporary hundreds of men suddenly entrusted to him for marching somewhere or other at the base. But Owen was quickly with his old battalion, and he obtained the command of D Company. His new experiences, as he had anticipated, were terrible, but he maintained the serenity of which he spoke, and he continued to write poems on the war. He wrote to Mr. Sassoon on September 22: "You said it would be a good thing for my poetry if I went back. That is my consolation for feeling a fool. This is what shells scream at me every time: 'Haven't you got the wits to keep out of this?'" And on October 10: "Your letter reached me at the exact moment it was most needed— when we had come far enough out of the line to feel the misery of billets; and I had been seized with writer's cramp after making out my casualty reports. (I'm O.C. D Coy.) The Battalion had a sheer time last week. I can find no better epithet; because I cannot say I suffered anything, having let my brain grow dull. That is to say, my nerves are in perfect order.

"It is a strange truth: that your *Counter-Attack* frightened me much more than the real one: though the boy by my side, shot through the head, lay on top of me, soaking my shoulder, for half an hour.

"Catalogue? Photograph? Can you photograph the crimson-hot iron as it cools from the smelting? That is what Jones's blood looked like, and felt like. My senses are charred.

"I shall feel again as soon as I dare, but now I must not. I don't take the cigarette out of my mouth when I write Deceased over their letters.
"But one day I will write Deceased over many books.

"I am glad I've been recommended for M.C., and hope I get it, for the confidence it may give me at home. Full of confidence after having taken a few machine-guns (with the help of one seraphic lance-corporal), I held a most glorious brief peace talk in a pill-box. You would have been *en pâmoisons.*" His Military Cross was duly awarded.

I quote further from the letter of October 10, 1918: "Yes, there is something you can send me: 2 copies of *Counter-Attack,* one inscribed. One is for the Adjutant—who begged a book of Erskine MacD.'s *Soldier-Poets* which I had with me—because I met one of these amalgamations at the Base. And liked him for his immediate subjugation to my principles and your mastery. . . . At the Base I met O'Riordan (of the Irish Theatre, and collaborator with Conrad). A troll of a man; not unlike Robbie (Ross) for unexpected shocks. It was easy, and, as I reflect, inevitable, to tell him everything about oneself. . . .While you are apparently given over to wrens, I have found brave companionship in a poppy, behind whose stalk I took cover from five machine-guns and several howitzers. I desire no more *exposed flanks* of any sort for a long time.

"Of many who promised to send me literary magazines no one has succeeded, except the Editor of *To-day.* . . .

A fellow officer, Lieut. J. Foulkes, M.C., has obligingly written down his reminiscences of the Owen who belonged to the trenches and billets of Flanders. "We travelled together (in company with Major Murphy, D.S.O., who was to become 2nd in Command, and, in early November, commanded the 2nd Manchesters) from the base, Étaples, to meet the Battalion at Corbie on the R. Ancre. . . .The first real attack in which we took part was the one which followed the capture of the Hindenburg Line. We had to take what I think was then looked upon as a 2nd Hindenburg Line and which I remember was well wired. The attack was successful but costly—Owen and I were the only officers left in our Company and he became *pro tem.* Company Commander. It was for his work here that he received the M.C. Left with few men and lacking any means of cover save a German pill-box, which was really a death-trap because it was on this that the enemy concentrated his fire, Owen succeeded in holding the line until relieved by the Lancs. Fusiliers some time afterwards. This is where I admired his work—in leading his remnants, in the middle of the night, back to safety. I remember feeling how glad I was that it was not my job to know how to get out. I was content to follow him with the utmost confidence in his leadership."

On October 29 he wrote, during the advance: "The civilians here are a wretched, dirty, crawling community, afraid of *us,* some of them, and no wonder, after the shelling we gave them three weeks ago. Did I tell you that five healthy girls died of fright in one night at the last village? The people in England and France who thwarted a peaceable retirement of the enemy from these areas are therefore now sacrificing aged French peasants and charming French children to our guns. Shells made by women in Birmingham are at this moment burying little children alive not very far from here. It is rumoured that Austria has really surrendered. The new soldiers cheer when they hear these rumours, but the old ones bite their pipes, and go on cleaning their rifles, unbelieving." On October 31 he described his company headquarters as "The Smoky Cellar of the Forester's House", and insisted on the happiness that he felt there, though "so thick is the smoke that I can hardly see by a candle 12 inches away, and so thick are the inmates that I can hardly write for pokes, nudges, and jolts."

Writing to his mother, Owen repeated the words, "My nerves are in perfect order. . . .I came out," he added, "in order to help these boys—directly by leading them as well as an officer can, indirectly by watching their sufferings that I may speak of them as well as a pleader can. I have done the first." He had, and he was to continue to the end, which came one week before the Armistice fell from heaven on those colourless and water-logged battle-fields. On November 4, 1918, in face of those resolute German machine-gunners who would not have yielded yet if they could have helped it, Wilfred Owen was endeavouring to pass his company over the Sambre Canal. "Zero," writes Mr. Foulkes, "was, I think, 6 A.M., and once more our Company was to lead. From the 'kicking-off trench' or road we reached the spot on the Canal which should have been temporarily bridged by the Engineers, but the plan had unfortunately failed owing to the heavy fire concentrated by machine-gunners and artillery at that particular spot. Instead of gaining the other side, we had therefore to take cover behind the Canal bank, which rose to a height of about four feet. Attempts were made to cross on rafts, but these were unsuccessful." Owen is remembered patting his men on the back as he moved about, with a "Well done!" and "You are doing very well, my boy". The Engineers who were trying to bridge the

Canal almost all became casualties. Owen took a hand with some duckboards or planks, and was at the water's edge helping his men to fix them when he was hit and killed. "The battalion eventually crossed lower down by means of a bridge near the village of Ors, a few miles south of Landrécies."

The indirect part of his sacrifice was then, for a brief moment, unnecessary. Peace came, men returned home, it seemed as though all the bugles in the world might blow without ever luring one of them again into the battle. But in a short time it was apparent that the peace was imperfect, and her olive-branch might easily turn into a rifle-grenade. We are not yet sure of ourselves. A threat hangs over us even now. The transmutation even of the European tragedy into a lending-library fashion shows anew how easy it is for humanity to follow a dream, and how hard it is for the romantic *Homo sapiens—the Homo rapiens* of Mr. H. S. Salt— to be a realist. In the coming race there will be a multitude of mirage-builders, and the business which now engages the heart and brain of so many leaders in every country is how to save them from the normal consequences of their own illusions, or those who, for whatever purpose, encourage and exploit them. Here Owen will be found achieving his object of pleading; being dead he speaks. He speaks as a soldier, with perfect and certain knowledge of war at grips with the soldier; as a mind, surveying the whole process of wasted spirit, art, and blood in all its instant and deeper evils; as a poet, giving his readers picture and tone that whenever they are reconsidered afford a fresh profundity, for they are combinations of profound recognitions.

He was, apart from Mr. Sassoon, the greatest of the English war poets. But the term 'war poets' is rather convenient than accurate. Wilfred Owen was a poet without classifications of war and peace. Had he lived, his humanity would have continued to encounter great and moving themes, the painful sometimes, sometimes the beautiful, and his art would have matched his vision. He was one of those destined beings who, without pride of self (the words of Shelley will never be excelled), "see, as from a tower, the end of all". Outwardly, he was quiet,* unobtrusive, full of good sense; inwardly, he could not help regarding the world with the dignity of a seer.

Owen was preparing himself to the last moment in experience, observation, and composition for a volume of poems, to strike at the conscience of England in regard to the continuance of the war. This volume had begun to take a definite form in his mind, which may be traced in the hastily written and obscurely amended Preface and Contents found among his papers. That they and his later poems exist at all in writing is, to all who knew, or realize, the fierce demands made on company officers in the front line and in its vicinity, a wonderful proof of his intellectual determination.

*"My impression was that nobody knew he was a poet. Save for some snatches of conversation between him and Captain Somerville, M.C., company commander in Corbie in September 1918, in which the names Sassoon, *Nation,* Athenæum were mentioned, I personally never dreamt of it." (Lieut. Foulkes)

PREFACE

This book is not about heroes.
English Poetry is not yet fit to speak of them.
Nor is it about deeds or lands, nor anything about
glory, honour, might, majesty, dominion or power,
except War.

Above all, this book is not concerned with Poetry.
The subject of it is War, and the pity of War.
The Poetry is in the pity.

Yet these elegies are not to this generation, in no sense consolatory.
They may be to the next.
All the poet can do to-day is to warn.
That is why the true Poets must be truthful.

(If I thought the letter of this book would last, I might have used proper names;
but if the spirit of it survives - survives Prussia, - my ambition and those names
will be content; for they will have achieved themselves fresher fields than
Flanders....)

*Note. This Preface was found, in an unfinished condition, among Wilfred
Owen's papers.*

WAR POEMS

Strange Meeting
1918.

It seemed that out of the battle I escaped
Down some profound dull tunnel, long since scooped
Through granites which Titanic wars had groined.
Yet also there encumbered sleepers groaned,
Too fast in thought or death to be bestirred.
Then, as I probed them, one sprang up, and stared
With piteous recognition in fixed eyes,
Lifting distressful hands as if to bless.
And by his smile, I knew that sullen hall,
By his dead smile I knew we stood in Hell.
With a thousand fears that vision's face was grained;
Yet no blood reached there from the upper ground,
And no guns thumped, or down the flues made moan.
"Strange, friend," I said, "Here is no cause to mourn."
"None," said the other, "Save the undone years,
The hopelessness. Whatever hope is yours,
Was my life also; I went hunting wild
After the wildest beauty in the world,
Which lies not calm in eyes, or braided hair,
But mocks the steady running of the hour,
And if it grieves, grieves richlier than here.
For of my glee might many men have laughed,
And of my weeping something has been left,
Which must die now. I mean the truth untold,
The pity of war, the pity war distilled.
Now men will go content with what we spoiled.
Or, discontent, boil bloody, and be spilled.
They will be swift with swiftness of the tigress.
None will break ranks, though nations trek from progress.
Courage was mine, and I had mystery;
Wisdom was mine, and I had mastery;
To miss the march of this retreating world
Into vain citadels that are not walled.
Then, when much blood had clogged their chariot-wheels,
I would go up and wash them from sweet wells,
Even with truths that lie too deep for taint.
I would have poured my spirit without stint

1

But not through wounds; not on the cess of war.
Foreheads of men have bled where no wounds were.
I am the enemy you killed, my friend.
I knew you in this dark: for so you frowned
Yesterday through me as you jabbed and killed.
I parried; but my hands were loath and cold.
Let us sleep now . . ."

psychological
scars of
war.

Insensibility

I

Happy are men who yet before they are killed
Can let their veins run cold.
Whom no compassion fleers
Or makes their feet
Sore on the alleys cobbled with their brothers.
The front line withers,
But they are troops who fade, not flowers
For poets' tearful fooling:
Men, gaps for filling:
Losses who might have fought
Longer; but no one bothers.

II

And some cease feeling
Even themselves or for themselves.
Dullness best solves
The tease and doubt of shelling,
And Chance's strange arithmetic
Comes simpler than the reckoning of their shilling.
They keep no check on armies' decimation.

III

Happy are these who lose imagination:
They have enough to carry with ammunition.
Their spirit drags no pack,
Their old wounds save with cold can not more ache.
Having seen all things red,
Their eyes are rid
Of the hurt of the colour of blood for ever.
And terror's first constriction over,
Their hearts remain small-drawn.
Their senses in some scorching cautery of battle
Now long since ironed,
Can laugh among the dying, unconcerned.

IV

Happy the soldier home, with not a notion
How somewhere, every dawn, some men attack,
And many sighs are drained.
Happy the lad whose mind was never trained:
His days are worth forgetting more than not.
He sings along the march
Which we march taciturn, because of dusk,
The long, forlorn, relentless trend
From larger day to huger night.

V

We wise, who with a thought besmirch
Blood over all our soul,
How should we see our task
But through his blunt and lashless eyes?
Alive, he is not vital overmuch;
Dying, not mortal overmuch;
Nor sad, nor proud,
Nor curious at all.
He cannot tell
Old men's placidity from his.

VI

But cursed are dullards whom no cannon stuns,
That they should be as stones;
Wretched are they, and mean
With paucity that never was simplicity.
By choice they made themselves immune
To pity and whatever mourns in man
Before the last sea and the hapless stars;
Whatever mourns when many leave these shores;
Whatever shares
The eternal reciprocity of tears.

Greater Love

Red lips are not so red
  As the stained stones kissed by the English dead.
Kindness of wooed and wooer
Seems shame to their love pure.
O Love, your eyes lose lure
  When I behold eyes blinded in my stead!

Your slender attitude
  Trembles not exquisite like limbs knife-skewed,
Rolling and rolling there
Where God seems not to care;
Till the fierce Love they bear
  Cramps them in death's extreme decrepitude.

Your voice sings not so soft, –
  Though even as wind murmuring through raftered loft, –
Your dear voice is not dear,
Gentle, and evening clear,
As theirs whom none now hear,
  Now earth has stopped their piteous mouths that coughed.

Heart, you were never hot
  Nor large, nor full like hearts made great with shot;
And though your hand be pale,
Paler are all which trail
Your cross through flame and hail:
  Weep, you may weep, for you may touch them not.

Apologia Pro Poemate Meo

I, too, saw God through mud—
    The mud that cracked on cheeks when wretches smiled.
    War brought more glory to their eyes than blood,
    And gave their laughs more glee than shakes a child.

Merry it was to laugh there—
    Where death becomes absurd and life absurder.
    For power was on us as we slashed bones bare
    Not to feel sickness or remorse of murder.

I, too, have dropped off fear—
    Behind the barrage, dead as my platoon,
    And sailed my spirit surging, light and clear
    Past the entanglement where hopes lay strewn;

And witnessed exultation—
    Faces that used to curse me, scowl for scowl,
    Shine and lift up with passion of oblation,
    Seraphic for an hour; though they were foul.

I have made fellowships—
    Untold of happy lovers in old song.
    For love is not the binding of fair lips
    With the soft silk of eyes that look and long,

By Joy, whose ribbon slips, —
    But wound with war's hard wire whose stakes are strong;
    Bound with the bandage of the arm that drips;
    Knit in the webbing of the rifle-thong.

I have perceived much beauty
    In the hoarse oaths that kept our courage straight;
    Heard music in the silentness of duty;
    Found peace where shell-storms spouted reddest spate.

Nevertheless, except you share
  With them in hell the sorrowful dark of hell,
  Whose world is but the trembling of a flare,
  And heaven but as the highway for a shell,

You shall not hear their mirth:
  You shall not come to think them well content
  By any jest of mine. These men are worth
  Your tears: You are not worth their merriment.

November 1917.

The Show

We have fallen in the dreams the ever-living
Breathe on the tarnished mirror of the world,
And then smooth out with ivory hands and sigh.
                              W B YEATS

My soul looked down from a vague height with Death,
As unremembering how I rose or why,
And saw a sad land, weak with sweats of dearth,
Gray, cratered like the moon with hollow woe,
And pitted with great pocks and scabs of plaques.

Across its beard, that horror of harsh wire,
There moved thin caterpillars, slowly uncoiled.
It seemed they pushed themselves to be as plugs
Of ditches, where they writhed and shrivelled, killed.

By them had slimy paths been trailed and scraped
Round myriad warts that might be little hills.

From gloom's last dregs these long-strung creatures crept,
And vanished out of dawn down hidden holes.

(And smell came up from those foul openings
As out of mouths, or deep wounds deepening.)

On dithering feet upgathered, more and more,
Brown strings towards strings of gray, with bristling spines,
All migrants from green fields, intent on mire.

Those that were gray, of more abundant spawns,
Ramped on the rest and ate them and were eaten.

I saw their bitten backs curve, loop, and straighten,
I watched those agonies curl, lift, and flatten.
Whereat, in terror what that sight might mean,
I reeled and shivered earthward like a feather.

And Death fell with me, like a deepening moan.
And He, picking a manner of worm, which half had hid
Its bruises in the earth, but crawled no further,
Showed me its feet, the feet of many men,
And the fresh-severed head of it, my head.

Mental Cases

Who are these? Why sit they here in twilight?
Wherefore rock they, purgatorial shadows,
Drooping tongues from jaws that slob their relish,
Baring teeth that leer like skulls' tongues wicked?
Stroke on stroke of pain, – but what slow panic,
Gouged these chasms round their fretted sockets?
Ever from their hair and through their hands' palms
Misery swelters. Surely we have perished
Sleeping, and walk hell; but who these hellish?

–These are men whose minds the Dead have ravished.
Memory fingers in their hair of murders,
Multitudinous murders they once witnessed.
Wading sloughs of flesh these helpless wander,
Treading blood from lungs that had loved laughter.
Always they must see these things and hear them,
Batter of guns and shatter of flying muscles,
Carnage incomparable and human squander
Rucked too thick for these men's extrication.

Therefore still their eyeballs shrink tormented
Back into their brains, because on their sense
Sunlight seems a blood-smear; night comes blood-black;
Dawn breaks open like a wound that bleeds afresh
–Thus their heads wear this hilarious, hideous,
Awful falseness of set-smiling corpses.
–Thus their hands are plucking at each other;
Picking at the rope-knouts of their scourging;
Snatching after us who smote them, brother,
Pawing us who dealt them war and madness.

The Parable of the Old Man and the Young

So Abram rose, and clave the wood, and went,
And took the fire with him, and a knife.
And as they sojourned both of them together,
Isaac the first-born spake and said, My Father,
Behold the preparations, fire and iron,
But where the lamb for this burnt-offering?
Then Abram bound the youth with belts and straps,
And builded parapets and trenches there,
And stretched forth the knife to slay his son.
When lo! an angel called him out of heaven,
Saying, Lay not thy hand upon the lad,
Neither do anything to him. Behold,
A ram caught in a thicket by its horns;
Offer the Ram of Pride instead of him.
But the old man would not so, but slew his son,
And half the seed of Europe, one by one.

Arms and the Boy

Let the boy try along this bayonet-blade
How cold steel is, and keen with hunger of blood;
Blue with all malice, like a madman's flash;
And thinly drawn with famishing for flesh.

Lend him to stroke these blind, blunt bullet-heads
Which long to muzzle in the hearts of lads.
Or give him cartridges of fine zinc teeth,
Sharp with the sharpness of grief and death.

For his teeth seem for laughing round an apple.
There lurk no claws behind his fingers supple;
And God will grow no talons at his heels,
Nor antlers through the thickness of his curls.

11

ordinarily
celebratory. *+personification*

SONNETS. A4DY

Anthem for Doomed Youth
1917.   *dehumani-sation*

What passing-bells for these who die as cattle?
  Only the monstrous anger of the guns.
  Only the stuttering rifles' rapid rattle →*onomatopoeia*
Can patter out their hasty orisons. *(prayer)*
No mockeries now for them; no prayers nor bells,
  Nor any voice of mourning save the choirs,— →*choirboys*
The shrill, demented choirs of wailing shells;   *going to war.*
  And bugles calling for them from sad shires.   *cries of death.*

link to title.

choirs.

What candles may be held to speed them all?
  Not in the hands of boys, but in their eyes
Shall shine the holy glimmers of goodbyes.
  The pallor of girls' brows shall be their pall; →*funerals;*
Their flowers the tenderness of patient minds,   *carrying*
And each slow dusk a drawing-down of blinds.   *the coffin*

→virginity?!

darken the house

rhythm fails: matching the breakdown of the young men's lives

religious imagery: everything preordained; predetermined deaths for them.

12

The Send-Off

Down the close, darkening lanes they sang their way
To the siding-shed,
And lined the train with faces grimly gay.

Their breasts were stuck all white with wreath and spray
As men's are, dead.

Dull porters watched them, and a casual tramp
Stood staring hard,
Sorry to miss them from the upland camp.
Then, unmoved, signals nodded, and a lamp
Winked to the guard.

So secretly, like wrongs hushed-up, they went.
They were not ours:
We never heard to which front these were sent.

Nor there if they yet mock what women meant
Who gave them flowers.

Shall they return to beatings of great bells
In wild trainloads?
A few, a few, too few for drums and yells,
May creep back, silent, to still village wells
Up half-known roads.

13

Dulce Et Decorum Est
1917

Bent double, like old beggars under sacks,
Knock-kneed, coughing like hags, we cursed through sludge,
Till on the haunting flares we turned our backs,
And towards our distant rest began to trudge.
Men marched asleep. Many had lost their boots
But limped on, blood-shod. All went lame, all blind;
Drunk with fatigue; deaf even to the hoots
Of gas-shells dropping softly behind.

Gas! GAS! Quick, boys! – An ecstasy of fumbling
Fitting the clumsy helmets just in time,
But someone still was yelling out and stumbling
And flound'ring like a man in fire or lime. . .
Dim through the misty panes and thick green light,
As under a green sea, I saw him drowning.

In all my dreams before my helpless sight
He plunges at me, guttering, choking, drowning.

If in some smothering dreams, you too could pace
Behind the wagon that we flung him in,
And watch the white eyes writhing in his face,
His hanging face, like a devil's sick of sin,
If you could hear, at every jolt, the blood
Come gargling from the froth-corrupted lungs,
Obscene as cancer, bitter as the cud
Of vile, incurable sores on innocent tongues, –
My friend, you would not tell with such high zest
To children ardent for some desperate glory,
The old Lie: Dulce et decorum est
Pro patria mori.

14

Handwritten annotations:

use of → young fit men reduced to this state.
v. old & v. young the frail; weakness.
⊕ 'boys' - fatherlike link to kist BB
dulce

the extremity of the terrain.

cry for help?

showing how they have become numbed.

juxtaposition of ideas.

sudden hit, not quoted - "reality" A0+ (see below)

now a warning
see last stanza; naivety.

desperation

never ending torment.

link: Great Gatsby: american dream; motivation

+tri-colon

put into the situation by government.

link: 1984 Winston's torture in No.1.

→ dehumanisation.

* word choice - cannot write/run 2nd person words said. introduces storytelling element.

unbearable agony

their tongues/ bodies being punished for the words of others.

its own commentary.

more than just age; naivety - know nothing of the world.
→ ecstacy: soldiers given stimulants to make them braver.

it is sweet & noble beautiful to die for your country.

- 4 quatrains
- alternate rhyme
- written in IABIC PENTAMETER -
× does not follow stress pattern.

makes the reader uncomfortable

Asleep

Under his helmet, up against his pack,
After so many days of work and waking,
Sleep took him by the brow and laid him back.
And in the happy no-time of his sleeping,
Death took him by the heart. There was a quaking
Of the aborted life within him leaping . . .
Then chest and sleepy arms once more fell slack.
And soon the slow, stray blood came creeping
From the intruding lead, like ants on track.

Whether his deeper sleep lie shaded by the shaking
Of great wings, and the thoughts that hung the stars,
High-pillowed on calm pillows of God's making,
Above these clouds, these rains, these sleets of lead,
And these winds' scimitars,
—Or whether yet his thin and sodden head
Confuses more and more with the low mould,
His hair being one with the grey grass
Of finished fields, and wire-scrags rusty-old,
Who knows? Who hopes? Who troubles? Let it pass!
He sleeps. He sleeps less tremulous, less cold
Than we who wake, and waking, say Alas!

The Sentry

We'd found an old Boche dug-out, and he knew,
And gave us hell, for shell on frantic shell
Hammered on top, but never quite burst through.
Rain, guttering down in waterfalls of slime
Kept slush waist high, that rising hour by hour,
Choked up the steps too thick with clay to climb.
What murk of air remained stank old, and sour
With fumes of whizz-bangs, and the smell of men
Who'd lived there years, and left their curse in the den,
If not their corpses. . . .
                              There we herded from the blast
Of whizz-bangs, but one found our door at last, –
Buffeting eyes and breath, snuffing the candles.
And thud! flump! thud! down the steep steps came thumping
And splashing in the flood, deluging muck –
The sentry's body; then his rifle, handles
Of old Boche bombs, and mud in ruck on ruck.
We dredged him up, for killed, until he whined
"O sir, my eyes – I'm blind – I'm blind, I'm blind!"
Coaxing, I held a flame against his lids
And said if he could see the least blurred light
He was not blind; in time he'd get all right.
"I can't," he sobbed. Eyeballs, huge-bulged like squids
Watch my dreams still; but I forgot him there
In posting next for duty, and sending a scout
To beg a stretcher somewhere, and floundering about
To other posts under the shrieking air.

                    *   *   *

Those other wretches, how they bled and spewed,
And one who would have drowned himself for good, –
I try not to remember these things now.
Let dread hark back for one word only: how
Half-listening to that sentry's moans and jumps,
And the wild chattering of his broken teeth,
Renewed most horribly whenever crumps
Pummelled the roof and slogged the air beneath –
Through the dense din, I say, we heard him shout
"I see your lights!" But ours had long died out.

16

The Dead-Beat

He dropped, – more sullenly than wearily,
Lay stupid like a cod, heavy like meat,
And none of us could kick him to his feet;
Just blinked at my revolver, blearily;
– Didn't appear to know a war was on,
Or see the blasted trench at which he stared.
"I'll do 'em in," he whined, "If this hand's spared,
I'll murder them, I will."

             A low voice said,
"It's Blighty, p'raps, he sees; his pluck's all gone,
Dreaming of all the valiant, that aren't dead:
Bold uncles, smiling ministerially;
Maybe his brave young wife, getting her fun
In some new home, improved materially.
It's not these stiffs have crazed him; nor the Hun."

We sent him down at last, out of the way.
Unwounded; – stout lad, too, before that strafe.
Malingering? Stretcher-bearers winked, "Not half!"

Next day I heard the Doc.'s well-whiskied laugh:
"That scum you sent last night soon died. Hooray!"

Exposure

Our brains ache, in the merciless iced east winds that knive us . . .
Wearied we keep awake because the night is silent . . .
Low drooping flares confuse our memory of the salient . . .
Worried by silence, sentries whisper, curious, nervous,
    But nothing happens.

Watching, we hear the mad gusts tugging on the wire,
Like twitching agonies of men among its brambles.
Northward incessantly, the flickering gunnery rumbles,
Far off, like a dull rumour of some other war.
    What are we doing here?

The poignant misery of dawn begins to grow . . .
We only know war lasts, rain soaks, and clouds sag stormy.
Dawn massing in the east her melancholy army
Attacks once more in ranks on shivering ranks of gray,
    But nothing happens.

Sudden successive flights of bullets streak the silence.
Less deadly than the air that shudders black with snow,
With sidelong flowing flakes that flock, pause and renew;
We watch them wandering up and down the wind's nonchalance,
    But nothing happens.

Pale flakes with lingering stealth come feeling for our faces –
We cringe in holes, back on forgotten dreams, and stare, snow-
dazed,
Deep into grassier ditches. So we drowse, sun-dozed,
Littered with blossoms trickling where the blackbird fusses.
    Is it that we are dying?

Slowly our ghosts drag home: glimpsing the sunk fires glozed
With crusted dark-red jewels; crickets jingle there;
For hours the innocent mice rejoice: the house is theirs;
Shutters and doors all closed: on us the doors are closed –
    We turn back to our dying.

18

Handwritten annotations:

- ¹ salient – part of trench in nomansland.
- ² knowledgable.
- total exposure to the elements.
- A rhyme scheme
- winds slowing; think. unable to
- constant waiting.
- line on its own; anti-climactic?
- almost a refrain
- whisper.
- wire itself become the new landscape.
- questioning in anger? or in patriotism.
- cleansing of dawn; metaphorical world fighting back against destruction
- language used; surrounding, contradicting
- dawn supposed to signify saviour, new day; men patriotic
- tri-color; demonstrating the realities of being on front line → heaviness
- prophetic fallacy
- metaphor – allied to dawn; new day of freedom
- alliteration – haunting
- assonance
- battle line.
- "cold gust... rumbled..." S.P.O. nature has affected them; elected them
- successive sky-motions.
- waiting for attack; further in to hopelessness.
- fires gone.
- break in the pattern used
- returning to earth, embraced by nature away from war; lying easy, "lying were at ease".
- memories; remembering / taken home not the same as before
- every one gone to war
- mourning.
- ** sibilance; contrasting what is being said – makes reader uncomfortable

innocent parts of nature.

Since we believe not otherwise can kind fires burn;
Now ever suns smile true on <u>child, or field, or fruit.</u>
For <u>God's invincible spring</u> our love is made afraid;
<u>Therefore, not loath, we lie out here;</u> <u>therefore were born,</u>
For <u>love of God seems dying.</u> — _Woodbine Willy_

God leading an army against those that destroyed everything.

To-night, (His) frost will fasten on this mud and us,
<u>Shrivelling many hands and puckering foreheads crisp.</u>
The burying-party, picks and shovels in their <u>shaking grasp.</u>
<u>Pause</u> over half-known faces. All their eyes are <u>ice,</u>
<u>But nothing happens.</u>

every part of nature abandoned/rebelled; now afraid of spring. — retaliation.

fear / ptsd / cold.

memories of war — retrain of before.

line coming in again — twisted irony — everything is happening; loss of life treated as nothing — common / not cared about —

remembering, mourning on front line; all the remembrance he'd recieve.

AO4 → propaganda & censorship of media. bad news not reported

19

Spring Offensive
1917

Halted against the shade of a last hill,
They fed, and, lying easy, were at ease
And, finding comfortable chests and knees,
Carelessly slept. But many there stood still
To face the stark, blank sky beyond the ridge,
Knowing their feet had come to the end of the world.

Marvelling they stood, and watched the long grass swirled
By the May breeze, murmurous with wasp and midge,
For though the summer oozed into their veins
Like the injected drug for their bones' pains,
Sharp on their souls hung the imminent line of grass,
Fearfully flashed the sky's mysterious glass.

Hour after hour they ponder the warm field–
And the far valley behind, where the buttercups
Had blessed with gold their slow boots coming up,
Where even the little brambles would not yield,
But clutched and clung to them like sorrowing hands;
They breathe like trees unstirred.

Till like a cold gust thrilled the little word
At which each body and its soul begird
And tighten them for battle. No alarms
Of bugles, no high flags, no clamorous haste–
Only a lift and flare of eyes that faced
The sun, like a friend with whom their love is done.
O larger shone that smile against the sun,–
Mightier than his whose bounty these have spurned.

So, soon they topped the hill, and raced together
Over an open stretch of herb and heather
Exposed. And instantly the whole sky burned
With fury against them; and soft sudden cups
Opened in thousands for their blood; and the green slopes
Chasmed and steepened sheer to infinite space

20

Of them who running on that last high place
Leapt to swift unseen bullets, or went up
On the hot blast and fury of hell's upsurge,
Or plunged and fell away past this world's verge,
Some say God caught them even before they fell.

But what say such as from existence' brink
Ventured but drave too swift to sink.
The few who rushed in the body to enter hell,
And there out-fiending all its fiends and flames
With superhuman inhumanities,
Long-famous glories, immemorial shames–
And crawling slowly back, have by degrees
Regained cool peaceful air in wonder–
Why speak they not of comrades that went under?

21

The Chances

I mind as 'ow the night afore that show
Us five got talkin', – we was in the know.
"Over the top to-morrer; boys, we're for it,
First wave we are, first ruddy wave; that's tore it."
"Ah well," says Jimmy, – an' 'e's seen some scrappin'–
"There ain't more nor five things as can 'appen;
Ye get knocked out; else wounded – bad or cushy;
Scuppered; or nowt except yer feelin' mushy."

One of us got the knock-out, blown to chops.
T'other was 'urt, like, losin' both 'is props.
An' one, to use the word of 'ypocrites,
'Ad the misfortoon to be took by Fritz.
Now me, I wasn't scratched, praise God Almighty
(Though next time please I'll thank 'im for a blighty),
But poor young Jim, 'e's livin' an' 'e's not;
'E reckoned 'e'd five chances, an' 'e 'ad;
'E's wounded, killed, and pris'ner, all the lot,
The bloody lot all rolled in one. Jim's mad.

S.I.W.*

> "I will to the King,
> And offer him consolation in his trouble,
> For that man there has set his teeth to die,
> And being one that hates obedience,
> Discipline, and orderliness of life,
> I cannot mourn him."
>
> W. B. Yeats.

I. THE PROLOGUE

Patting goodbye, doubtless they told the lad
He'd always show the Hun a brave man's face;
Father would sooner him dead than in disgrace,–
Was proud to see him going, aye, and glad.
Perhaps his Mother whimpered how she'd fret
Until he got a nice, safe wound to nurse.
Sisters would wish girls too could shoot, charge, curse;
Brothers – would send his favourite cigarette,
Each week, month after month, they wrote the same,
Thinking him sheltered in some Y.M. Hut,
Because he said so, writing on his butt
Where once an hour a bullet missed its aim   →romeo
And misses teased the hunger of his brain.   &juliet quote
His eyes grew old with wincing, and his hand
Reckless with ague. Courage leaked, as sand
From the best sandbags after years of rain.
But never leave, wound, fever, trench-foot, shock,
Untrapped the wretch. And death seemed still withheld
For torture of lying machinally shelled,
At the pleasure of this world's Powers who'd run amok.

He'd seen men shoot their hands, on night patrol,
Their people never knew. Yet they were vile.
"Death sooner than dishonour, that's the style!"
So Father said.

II. THE ACTION

One dawn, our wire patrol
ed him. This time, Death had not missed.
ould do nothing, but wipe his bleeding cough.
d it be accident? – Rifles go off . . .
sniped? No. (Later they found the English ball.)

Yeats Quote.

23

III. THE POEM
It was the reasoned crisis of his soul.
Against the fires that would not burn him whole
But kept him for death's perjury and scoff
And life's half-promising, and both their riling.

IV. THE EPILOGUE
With him they buried the muzzle his teeth had kissed,
And truthfully wrote the Mother "Tim died smiling".

* *Self-inflicted wound.*

Futility
1918

Move him into the sun–
Gently its touch awoke him once,
At home, whispering of fields unsown.
Always it woke him, even in France,
Until this morning and this snow.
If anything might rouse him now
The kind old sun will know.

Think how it wakes the seeds–
Woke, once, the clays of a cold star.
Are limbs so dear-achieved, are sides
Full-nerved, – still warm, – too hard to stir?
Was it for this the clay grew tall?
– O what made fatuous sunbeams toil
To break earth's sleep at all?

[Handwritten annotations surrounding the poem:]

broken
structure – broken men

disturbed —
lives nothing ever half rhymes
goes to
plan of disrupt
normal
rhythm

dulce - contrast.
"Hung into
a wagon"

elegiac
mournful
of song

No
longer there ...
so much
question duties
of

repetitions;
moment of death,
specifically this man

if the sun
can wake the
earth, why
can it not
wake one
man?

sun ack to
awake life
emphasis

human form
perfection of
one
God.

basis
of
humanity.

of
turning
against
natural God,
earth no
longer sacred
but God.

break;
frustrating creating life
moment to destroy it.
of
emotion

foolish.

Wordsworth:
upon
Westminster
Bridge;
exclamative
in final
lines.

25

The Last Laugh
1918

'Oh! Jesus Christ! I'm hit,' he said; and died.
Whether he vainly cursed or prayed indeed,
The Bullets chirped–In vain, vain, vain!
Machine-guns chuckled, –Tut-tut! Tut-tut!
And the Big Gun guffawed.

Another sighed,–'O Mother, mother! Dad!'
Then smiled at nothing, childlike, being dead.
    And the lofty Shrapnel-cloud
    Leisurely gestured, –Fool!
    And the splinters spat, and tittered.

'My Love!' one moaned. Love-languid seemed his mood,
Till slowly lowered, his whole faced kissed the mud.
    And the Bayonets' long teeth grinned;
    Rabbles of Shells hooted and groaned;
    And the Gas hissed.

The Letter

With B.E.F. Jun 10. Dear Wife,
(Oh blast this pencil. 'Ere, Bill, lend's a knife.)
I'm in the pink at present, dear.
I think the war will end this year.
We don't see much of them square-'eaded 'Uns.
We're out of harm's way, not bad fed.
I'm longing for a taste of your old buns.
(Say, Jimmie, spare's a bite of bread.)
There don't seem much to say just now.
(Yer what? Then don't, yer ruddy cow!
And give us back me cigarette!)
I'll soon be 'ome. You mustn't fret.
My feet's improvin', as I told you of.
We're out in the rest now. Never fear.
(VRACH! By crumbs, but that was near.)
Mother might spare you half a sov.
Kiss Nell and Bert. When me and you–
(Eh? What the 'ell! Stand to? Stand to!
Jim, give's a hand with pack on, lad.
Guh! Christ! I'm hit. Take 'old. Aye, bad.
No, damn your iodine. Jim? 'Ere!
Write my old girl, Jim, there's a dear.)

Smile, Smile, Smile

Head to limp head, the sunk-eyed wounded scanned
Yesterday's *Mail*; the casualties (typed small)
And (large) Vast Booty from our Latest Haul.
Also, they read of Cheap Homes, not yet planned;
"For," said the paper, "when this war is done
The men's first instinct will be making homes.
Meanwhile their foremost need is aerodromes,
It being certain war has just begun.
Peace would do wrong to our undying dead,–
The sons we offered might regret they died
If we got nothing lasting in their stead.
We must be solidly indemnified.
Though all be worthy Victory which all bought,
We rulers sitting in this ancient spot
Would wrong our very selves if we forgot
The greatest glory will be theirs who fought,
Who kept this nation in integrity."
Nation? The half-limbed readers did not chafe
But smiled at one another curiously
Like secret men who know their secret safe.
(This is the thing they know and never speak,
That England one by one had fled to France
Not many elsewhere now save under France.)
Pictures of these broad smiles appear each week,
And people in whose voice real feeling rings
Say: How they smile! They're happy now, poor things.

23rd September 1918.

[Handwritten annotations:]
not given the attention deserved.
propaganda
everything came to nothing; accumulation of
glory of war
the ultimate sacrifice.
irony
question of national identity; pride in England.
away from home in pursuing glory.
now dead in France
now brushing over the hopelessness of the war.
no scars of war.

A03

Conscious

His fingers wake, and flutter up the bed.
His eyes come open with a pull of will,
Helped by the yellow may-flowers by his head.
A blind-cord drawls across the window-sill . . .
How smooth the floor of the ward is! what a rug!
And who's that talking, somewhere out of sight?
Why are they laughing? What's inside that jug?
"Nurse! Doctor!" – "Yes; all right, all right."

But sudden dusk bewilders all the air–
There seems no time to want a drink of water,
Nurse looks so far away. And here and there
Music and roses burnt through crimson slaughter.
He can't remember where he saw blue sky.
More blankets. Cold. He's cold. And yet so hot.
And there's no light to see the voices by;
No time to ask – he knows not what.

A Terre

(BEING THE PHILOSOPHY OF MANY SOLDIERS)

Sit on the bed; I'm blind, and three parts shell.
Be careful; can't shake hands now; never shall.
Both arms have mutinied against me – brutes.
My fingers fidget like ten idle brats.

I tried to peg out soldierly,–no use!
One dies of war like any old disease.
This bandage feels like pennies on my eyes.
I have my medals? – Discs to make eyes close.
My glorious ribbons? – Ripped from my own back
In scarlet shreds. (That's for your poetry book.)

A short life and a merry one, my buck!
We used to say we'd hate to live dead-old,–
Yet now . . . I'd willingly be puffy, bald,
And patriotic. Buffers catch from boys
At least the jokes hurled at them. I suppose
Little I'd ever teach a son, but hitting,
Shooting, war, hunting, all the arts of hurting.
Well, that's what I learnt, – that, and making money.

Your fifty years ahead seem none too many?
Tell me how long I've got? God! For one year
To help myself to nothing more than air!
One Spring! Is one too good to spare, too long?
Spring wind would work its own way to my lung,
And grow me legs as quick as lilac-shoots.

My servant's lamed, but listen how he shouts!
When I'm lugged out, he'll still be good for that.
Here in this mummy-case, you know, I've thought
How well I might have swept his floors for ever.
I'd ask no nights off when the bustle's over,
Enjoying so the dirt. Who's prejudiced
Against a grimed hand when his own's quite dust,
Less live than specks that in the sun-shafts turn,
Less warm than dust that mixes with arms' tan?
I'd love to be a sweep, now, black as Town,

Yes, or a muckman. Must I be his load?

O Life, Life, let me breathe,–a dug-out rat!
Not worse than ours the existences rats lead–
Nosing along at night down some safe rut,
They find a shell-proof home before they rot.
Dead men may envy living mites in cheese,
Or good germs even. Microbes have their joys,
And subdivide, and never come to death.
Certainly flowers have the easiest time on earth.
"I shall be one with nature, herb, and stone."
Shelley would tell me. Shelley would be stunned:
The dullest Tommy hugs that fancy now.
"Pushing up daisies," is their creed, you know.
To grain, then, go my fat, to buds my sap,
For all the usefulness there is in soap.
D'you think the Boche will ever stew man-soup?
Some day, no doubt, if . . .

         Friend, be very sure
I shall be better off with plants that share
More peaceably the meadow and the shower.
Soft rains will touch me, – as they could touch once,
And nothing but the sun shall make me ware.
Your guns may crash around me. I'll not hear;
Or, if I wince, I shall not know I wince.
Don't take my soul's poor comfort for your jest.
Soldiers may grow a soul when turned to fronds,
But here the thing's best left at home with friends.

My soul's a little grief, grappling your chest,
To climb your throat on sobs; easily chased
On other sighs and wiped by fresher winds.

Carry my crying spirit till it's weaned
To do without what blood remained these wounds.

Wild With All Regrets

My arms have mutinied against me – brutes!
My fingers fidget like ten idle brats,
My back's been stiff for hours, damned hours.
Death never gives his squad a Stand-at-ease.
I can't read. There: it's no use. Take your book.
A short life and a merry one, my buck!
We said we'd hate to grow dead-old. But now,
Not to live old seems awful: not to renew
My boyhood with my boys, and teach 'em hitting,
Shooting and hunting, – all the arts of hurting!
–Well, that's what I learnt. That, and making money.
Your fifty years in store seem none too many,
But I've five minutes. God! For just two years
To help myself to this good air of yours!
One Spring! Is one too hard to spare? Too long?
Spring air would find its own way to my lung,
And grow me legs as quick as lilac-shoots.

Yes, there's the orderly. He'll change the sheets
When I'm lugged out, oh, couldn't I do that?
Here in this coffin of a bed, I've thought
I'd like to kneel and sweep his floors for ever,–
And ask no nights off when the bustle's over,
For I'd enjoy the dirt; who's prejudiced
Against a grimed hand when his own's quite dust,–
Less live than specks that in the sun shafts turn?
Dear dust–in rooms, on roads, on faces' tan!
I'd love to be a sweep's boy, black as Town;
Yes, or a muck-man. Must I be his load?
A flea would do. If one chap wasn't bloody,
Or went stone-cold, I'd find another body.

Which I shan't manage now. Unless it's yours.
I shall stay in you, friend, for some few hours.
You'll feel my heavy spirit chill your chest,
And climb your throat on sobs, until it's chased
On sighs, and wiped from off your lips by wind.
I think on your rich breathing, brother, I'll be weaned
To do without what blood remained me from my wound.

5th December 1917.

Disabled

1917

He sat in a wheeled chair, waiting for dark,
And shivered in his ghastly suit of grey,
Legless, sewn short at elbow. Through the park
Voices of boys rang saddening like a hymn,
Voices of play and pleasure after day,
Till gathering sleep had mothered them from him.

About this time Town used to swing so gay
When glow-lamps budded in the light-blue trees
And girls glanced lovelier as the air grew dim,–
In the old times, before he threw away his knees.
Now he will never feel again how slim
Girls' waists are, or how warm their subtle hands;
All of them touch him like some queer disease.

There was an artist silly for his face,
For it was younger than his youth, last year.
Now he is old; his back will never brace;
He's lost his colour very far from here,
Poured it down shell-holes till the veins ran dry,
And half his lifetime lapsed in the hot race,
And leap of purple spurted from his thigh.

One time he liked a bloodsmear down his leg,
After the matches carried shoulder-high.
It was after football, when he'd drunk a peg,
He thought he'd better join.–He wonders why.
Someone had said he'd look a god in kilts.
That's why; and maybe, too, to please his Meg;
Aye, that was it, to please the giddy jilts,
He asked to join. He didn't have to beg;
Smiling they wrote his lie; aged nineteen years.
Germans he scarcely thought of; all their guilt,
And Austria's, did not move him. And no fears
Of Fear came yet. He thought of jewelled hilts
For daggers in plaid socks; of smart salutes;
And care of arms; and leave; and pay arrears;
Esprit de corps; and hints for young recruits.
And soon, he was drafted out with drums and cheers.

33

Some cheered him home, but not as crowds cheer Goal.
Only a solemn man who brought him fruits
Thanked him; and then inquired about his soul.

Now, he will spend a few sick years in Institutes,
And do what things the rules consider wise,
And take whatever pity they may dole.
To-night he noticed how the women's eyes
Passed from him to the strong men that were whole.
How cold and late it is! Why don't they come
And put him into bed? Why don't they come?

Inspection

"You! What d'you mean by this?" I rapped.
"You dare come on parade like this?"
"Please, sir, it's–" "'Old yer mouth," the sergeant snapped.
"I takes 'is name, sir?" –"Please, and then dismiss."

Some days "confined to camp" he got,
For being "dirty on parade".
He told me, afterwards, the damnèd spot
Was blood, his own. "Well, blood is dirt," I said.

"Blood's dirt," he laughed, looking away,
Far off to where his wound had bled
And almost merged for ever into clay.
"The world is washing out its stains," he said.
"It doesn't like our cheeks so red:
Young blood's its great objection.
But when we're duly white-washed, being dead,
The race will bear Field-Marshal God's inspection."

The Calls

A dismal fog-hoarse siren howls at dawn.
I watch the man it calls for, pushed and drawn
Backwards and forwards, helpless as a pawn.
    But I'm lazy, and his work's crazy.

Quick treble bells begin at nine o'clock,
Scuttling the schoolboy pulling up his sock,
Scaring the late girl in the inky frock.
    I must be crazy; I learn from the daisy.

Stern bells annoy the rooks and doves at ten.
I watch the verger close the doors, and when
I hear the organ moan the first amen,
    Sing my religion's—same as pigeons'.

A blatant bugle tears my afternoons.
Out clump the clumsy Tommies by platoons,
Trying to keep in step with rag-time tunes,
    But I sit still; I've done my drill.

Gongs hum and buzz like saucepan-lids at dusk,
I see a food-hog whet his gold-filled tusk
To eat less bread, and more luxurious rusk.

Then sometimes late at night my window bumps
From gunnery-practice, till my small heart thumps
And listens for the shell-shrieks and the crumps,
    But that's not all.

For leaning out last midnight on my sill
I heard the sighs of men, that have no skill
To speak of their distress, no, nor the will!
    A voice I know. And this time I must go.

At a Calvary Near The Ancre

One ever hangs where shelled roads part.
    In this war He too lost a limb,
But His disciples hide apart;
    And now the Soldiers bear with Him.

Near Golgotha strolls many a priest,
    And in their faces there is pride
That they were flesh-marked by the Beast
    By whom the gentle Christ's denied.

The scribes on all the people shove
    And bawl allegiance to the state,
But they who love the greater love
    Lay down their life; they do not hate.

[A "Calvary" is a statue of the crucified Christ; these crucifixes are erected at many crossroads in France.]

Le Christianisme

So the church Christ was hit and buried
      Under its rubbish and its rubble.
In cellars, packed-up saints lie serried,
      Well out of hearing of our trouble.

One Virgin still immaculate
      Smiles on for war to flatter her.
She's halo'd with an old tin hat
      But a piece of hell will batter her.

QUIVIÈRES.

Soldier's Dream

I dreamed kind Jesus fouled the big-gun gears;
And caused a permanent stoppage in all bolts;
And buckled with a smile Mausers and Colts;
And rusted every bayonet with His tears.

And there were no more bombs, of ours or Theirs,
Not even an old flint-lock, nor even a pikel.
But God was vexed, and gave all power to Michael;
And when I woke he'd seen to our repairs.

An early version written in October, 1917.

I dreamed that Christ had fouled the big-gun gears,
And made a permanent stoppage in all bolts
And buckled, with a smile, Mausers and Colts,
And rusted every bayonet with His tears.

And there were no more bombs, of ours or Theirs.
So we got out, and gathering up our plunder
Of pains, and nightmares for the night, in wonder!—
Leapt the communication trench like flares.

But at the port, a man from U.S.A.
Stopped us, and said: You go right back this minute.
I'll follow. Christ, your miracle ain't in it,
I'll get those rifles mended by today.

Sonnet

ON SEEING A PIECE OF OUR ARTILLERY BROUGHT INTO ACTION

Be slowly lifted up, thou long black arm,
Great gun towering towards Heaven, about to curse;
Sway steep against them, and for years rehearse
Huge imprecations like a blasting charm!
Reach at that Arrogance which needs thy harm,
And beat it down before its sins grow worse;
Spend our resentment, cannon,—yea, disburse
Our gold in shapes of flame, our breaths in storm.

Yet, for men's sakes whom thy vast malison
Must wither innocent of enmity,
Be not withdrawn, dark arm, thy spoilure done,
Safe to the bosom of our prosperity.
But when thy spell be cast complete and whole,
May God curse thee, and cut thee from our soul!

The Next War

War's a joke for me and you,
While we know such dreams are true.
                SIEGFRIED SASSOON

Out there, we've walked quite friendly up to Death;
    Sat down and eaten with him, cool and bland,—
    Pardoned his spilling mess-tins in our hand.
We've sniffed the green thick odour of his breath,—
Our eyes wept, but our courage didn't writhe.
    He's spat at us with bullets and he's coughed
    Shrapnel. We chorussed when he sang aloft;
We whistled while he shaved us with his scythe.

Oh, Death was never enemy of ours!
    We laughed at him, we leagued with him, old chum.
No soldier's paid to kick against his powers.
    We laughed, knowing that better men would come,
And greater wars; when each proud fighter brags
He wars on Death—for lives; not men—for flags.

OTHER POEMS AND FRAGMENTS

The End

After the blast of lightning from the east,
The flourish of loud clouds, the Chariot Throne;
After the drums of time have rolled and ceased,
And by the bronze west long retreat is blown,

Shall Life renew these bodies? Of a truth
All death will he annul, all tears assuage?—
Or fill these void veins full again with youth,
And wash with an immortal water, Age?

When I do ask white Age, he saith not so,
"My head hangs weighed with snow."
And when I hearken to the Earth she saith:
My fiery heart shrinks aching. It is death
Mine ancient scars shall not be glorified,
Nor my titanic tears, the seas be dried."

The Unreturning

Suddenly night crushed out the day and hurled
Her remnants over cloud-peaks, thunder-walled.
Then fell a stillness such as harks appalled
When far-gone dead return upon the world.

There watched I for the Dead; but no ghost woke.
Each one whom Life exiled I named and called.
But they were all too far, or dumbed, or thralled,
And never one fared back to me or spoke.

Then peered the indefinite unshapen dawn
With vacant gloaming, sad as half-lit minds,
The weak-limned hour when sick men's sighs are drained.
And while I wondered on their being withdrawn,
Gagged by the smothering wing which none unbinds,   `
I dreaded even a heaven with doors so chained.

Miners

There was a whispering in my hearth,
    A sigh of the coal,
Grown wistful of a former earth
    It might recall.

I listened for a tale of leaves
    And smothered ferns;
Frond-forests; and the low, sly lives
    Before the fawns.

My fire might show steam-phantoms simmer
    From Time's old cauldron,
Before the birds made nests in summer,
    Or men had children.

But the coals were murmuring of their mine,
    And moans down there
Of boys that slept wry sleep, and men
    Writhing for air.

And I saw white bones in the cinder-shard.
    Bones without number;
For many hearts with coal are charred
    And few remember.

I thought of some who worked dark pits
    Of war, and died
Digging the rock where Death reputes
    Peace lies indeed.

Comforted years will sit soft-chaired
    In rooms of amber;
The years will stretch their hands, well-cheered
    By our lives' ember.

The centuries will burn rich loads
    With which we groaned,
Whose warmth shall lull their dreaming lids
    While songs are crooned.
But they will not dream of us poor lads
    Lost in the ground.

Happiness

Ever again to breathe pure happiness,
The happiness our mother gave us, boys?
To smile at nothings, needing no caress?
Have we not laughed too often since with joys?
Have we not wrought too sick and sorrowful wrongs
For her hands' pardoning? The sun may cleanse,
And time, and starlight. Life will sing sweet songs,
And gods will show us pleasures more than men's.

Yet heaven looks smaller than the old doll's-home,
No nestling place is left in bluebell bloom,
And the wide arms of trees have lost their scope.
The former happiness is unreturning:
Boys' griefs are not so grievous as our yearning,
Boys have no sadness sadder than our hope.

Shadwell Stair

I am the ghost of Shadwell Stair.
    Along the wharves by the water-house,
    And through the dripping slaughter-house,
I am the shadow that walks there.

Yet I have flesh both firm and cool,
    And eyes tumultuous as the gems
    Of moons and lamps in the lapping Thames
When dusk sails wavering down the pool.

Shuddering the purple street-arc burns
    Where I watch always; from the banks
    Dolorously the shipping clanks,
And after me a strange tide turns.

I walk till the stars of London wane
    And dawn creeps up the Shadwell Stair.
    But when the crowing syrens blare
I with another ghost am lain.

Six o'clock in Princes Street

In twos and threes, they have not far to roam,
  Crowds that thread eastward, gay of eyes;
Those seek no further than their quiet home,
  Wives, walking westward, slow and wise.

Neither should I go fooling over clouds,
  Following gleams unsafe, untrue,
And tiring after beauty through star-crowds,
  Dared I go side by side with you;

Or be you in the gutter where you stand,
  Pale rain-flawed phantom of the place,
With news of all the nations in your hand,
  And all their sorrows in your face.

The Roads Also

The roads also have their wistful rest,
When the weathercocks perch still and roost,
And the town is a candle-lit room—
The streets also dream their dream.

The old houses muse of the old days
And their fond trees leaning on them doze,
On their steps chatter and clatter stops,
On their doors a strange hand taps.

Men remember alien ardours
As the dusk unearths old mournful odours.
In the garden unborn child souls wail
And the dead scribble on walls.

Though their own child cry for them in tears,
Women weep but hear no sound upstairs.
They believe in loves they had not lived
And in passion past the reach of the stairs
To the world's towers or stars.

Hospital Barge at Cérisy

Budging the sluggard ripples of the Somme,
A barge round old Cérisy slowly slewed.
Softly her engines down the current screwed
And chuckled in her, with contented hum.

Till fairy tinklings struck their croonings dumb.
The waters rumpling at the stern subdued.
The lock-gate took her bulging amplitude.
Gently from out the gurgling lock she swum.

One reading by that sunset raised his eyes
To watch her lessening westward quietly,
Till, as she neared the bend, her funnel screamed.

And that long lamentation made him wise
How unto Avalon, in agony,
Kings passed in the dark barge,
which Merlin dreamed.

December 8, 1917.

Training

Not this week nor this month dare I lie down
In languor under lime trees or smooth smile.
Love must not kiss my face pale that is brown.

My lips, parting, shall drink space, mile by mile;
Strong meats be all my hunger; my renown
Be the clean beauty of speed and pride of style.

Cold winds encountered on the racing Down
Shall thrill my heated bareness; but awhile
None else may meet me till I wear my crown.

June 1918.

Sonnet

Sweet is your antique body, not yet young.
Beauty withheld from youth that looks for youth.
Fair only for your father. Dear among
Masters in art. To all men else uncouth
Save me, who know your smile comes very old,
Learnt of the happy dead that laughed with gods;
For earlier suns than ours have lent you gold,
Sly fauns and trees have given you jigs and nods.

But soon your heart, hot-beating like a bird's,
Shall slow down. Youth shall lop your hair,
And you must learn wry meanings in our words.
Your smile shall dull, because too keen aware;
And when for hopes your hand shall be uncurled,
Your eyes shall close, being opened to the world.

To Eros

In that I loved you, Love, I worshipped you.
In that I worshipped well, I sacrificed.
All of most worth I bound and burnt and slew:
Old peaceful lives; frail flowers; firm friends; and Christ.

I slew all falser loves; I slew all true,
That I might nothing love but your truth, Boy.
Fair fame I cast away as bridegrooms do
Their wedding garments in their haste of joy.

But when I fell upon your sandalled feet,
You laughed; you loosed away my lips; you rose.
I heard the singing of your wings' retreat;
Far-flown, I watched you flush the Olympian snows,
Beyond my hoping. Starkly I returned
To stare upon the ash of all I burned.

My Shy Hand

My shy hand shades a hermitage apart,
    O large enough for thee, and thy brief hours.
Life there is sweeter held than in God's heart,
    Stiller than in the heavens of hollow flowers.

The wine is gladder there than in gold bowls.
    And Time shall not drain thence, nor trouble spill.
Sources between my fingers feed all souls,
    Where thou mayest cool thy lips, and draw thy fill.

Five cushions hath my hand, for reveries;
    And one deep pillow for thy brow's fatigues;
Languor of June all winterlong, and ease
    For ever from the vain untravelled leagues.

Thither your years may gather in from storm,
And Love, that sleepeth there, will keep thee warm.

The Kind Ghosts

She sleeps on soft, last breaths; but no ghost looms
Out of the stillness of her palace wall,
Her wall of boys on boys and dooms on dooms.

She dreams of golden gardens and sweet glooms,
Not marvelling why her roses never fall
Nor what red mouths were torn to make their blooms.

The shades keep down which well might roam her hall.
Quiet their blood lies in her crimson rooms
And she is not afraid of their footfall.

They move not from her tapestries, their pall,
Nor pace her terraces, their hecatombs,
Lest aught she be disturbed, or grieved at all.

July 30, 1918.

Winter Song

The browns, the olives, and the yellows died,
And were swept up to heaven; where they glowed
Each dawn and set of sun till Christmastide,
And when the land lay pale for them, pale-snowed,
Fell back, and down the snow-drifts flamed and flowed.

From off your face, into the winds of winter,
The sun-brown and the summer-gold are blowing;
But they shall gleam again with spiritual glinter,
When paler beauty on your brows falls snowing,
And through those snows my looks shall be soft-going.

October 18, 1917.

Music

I have been urged by earnest violins
And drunk their mellow sorrows to the slake
Of all my sorrows and my thirsting sins.
My heart has beaten for a brave drum's sake.
Huge chords have wrought me mighty: I have hurled
Thuds of God's thunder. And with old winds pondered
Over the curse of this chaotic world,—
With low lost winds that maundered as they wandered.

I have been gay with trivial fifes that laugh;
And songs more sweet than possible things are sweet;
And gongs, and oboes. Yet I guessed not half
Life's symphony till I had made hearts beat,
And touched Love's body into trembling cries,
And blown my love's lips into laughs and sighs.

October 1916-1917.

Storm

His face was charged with beauty as a cloud
With glimmering lightning. When it shadowed me
I shook, and was uneasy as a tree
That draws the brilliant danger, tremulous, bowed.

So must I tempt that face to loose its lightning.
Great gods, whose beauty is death, will laugh above,
Who made his beauty lovelier than love.
I shall be bright with their unearthly brightening.

And happier were it if my sap consume;
Glorious will shine the opening of my heart;
The land shall freshen that was under gloom;
What matter if all men cry aloud and start,
And women hide bleak faces in their shawl,
At those hilarious thunders of my fall?

October 1916.

To My Friend

(WITH AN IDENTITY DISC)

If ever I had dreamed of my dead name
    High in the heart of London, unsurpassed
By Time for ever, and the Fugitive, Fame,
    There seeking a long sanctuary at last,—

Or if I onetime hoped to hide its shame,
    —Shame of success, and sorrow of defeats,—
Under those holy cypresses, the same
    That shade always the quiet place of Keats,

Now rather thank I God there is no risk
    Of gravers scoring it with florid screed.
Let my inscription be this soldier's disc. . . .
    Wear it, sweet friend. Inscribe no date nor deed.
But may thy heart-beat kiss it, night and day,
Until the name grow blurred and fade away.

Fragment: Not One Corner ...

Not one corner of a foreign field
But a span as wide as Europe,
Deep as [   ].
I looked and saw.
An appearance of a titan's grave,
And the length thereof a thousand miles.
It crossed all Europe like a mystic road,
Or as the Spirits' Pathway lieth on the night.
And I heard a voice crying,
This is the Path of Glory.

Fragment: Cramped in that Funnelled Hole

Cramped in that funnelled hole, they watched the dawn
Open a jagged rim around; a yawn
Of death's jaws, which had all but swallowed them
Stuck in the bottom of his throat of phlegm.

They were in one of many mouths of Hell
Not seen of seers in visions; only felt
As teeth of traps; when bones and the dead are smelt
Under the mud where long ago they fell
Mixed with the sour sharp odour of the shell.

Fragment: I saw his Round Mouth's Crimson...

I saw his round mouth's crimson deepen as it fell,
　　Like a Sun, in his last deep hour;
Watched the magnificent recession of farewell,
　　Clouding, half gleam, half glower,
And a last splendour burn the heavens of his cheek.
　　And in his eyes
The cold stars lighting, very old and bleak,
　　In different skies.

Fragment: As Bronze may be much Beautified

As bronze may be much beautified
By lying in the dark damp soil,
So men who fade in dust of warfare fade
Fairer, and sorrow blooms their soul.

Like pearls which noble women wear
And, tarnishing, awhile confide
Unto the old salt sea to feed,
Many return more lustrous than they were.

But what of them buried profound,
Buried where we can no more find,
Who [   ]
Lie dark for ever under abysmal war?

Has Your Soul Sipped?

Has your soul sipped
      Of the sweetness of all sweets?
Has it well supped
      But yet hungers and sweats?

I have been witness
      Of a strange sweetness,
All fancy surpassing
      Past all supposing.

Passing the rays
      Of the rubies of morning,
Or the soft rise
      Of the moon; or the meaning
Known to the rose
      Of her mystery and mourning.

Sweeter than nocturnes
      Of the wild nightingale
Or than love's nectar
      After life's gall.

Sweeter than odours
      Of living leaves,
Sweeter than ardours
      Of dying loves.

Sweeter than death
      And dreams hereafter
To one in dearth
      Of life and its laughter.

Or the proud wound
      The victor wears
Or the last end
      Of all wars.

Or the sweet murder
    After long guard
Unto the martyr
    Smiling at God;

To me was that Smile,
    Faint as a wan, worn myth,
Faint and exceeding small,
    On a boy's murdered mouth.

Though from his throat
    The life-tide leaps
There was no threat
    On his lips.

But with the bitter blood
    And the death-smell
All his life's sweetness bled
    Into a smile.

MINOR POEMS, AND JUVENILIA

From My Diary, July 1914

Leaves
    Murmuring by myriads in the shimmering trees.
Lives
    Wakening with wonder in the Pyrenees.
Birds
    Cheerily chirping in the early day.
Bards
    Singing of summer, scything thro' the hay.
Bees
    Shaking the heavy dews from bloom and frond.
Boys
    Bursting the surface of the ebony pond.
Flashes
    Of swimmers carving thro' the sparkling cold.
Fleshes
    Gleaming with wetness to the morning gold.
A mead
    Bordered about with warbling water brooks.
A maid
    Laughing the love-laugh with me; proud of looks.
The heat
    Throbbing between the upland and the peak.
Her heart
    Quivering with passion to my pressed cheek.
Braiding
    Of floating flames across the mountain brow.
Brooding
    Of stillness; and a sighing of the bough.
Stirs
    Of leaflets in the gloom; soft petal-showers;
Stars
    Expanding with the starr'd nocturnal flowers.

On My Songs

Though unseen Poets, many and many a time,
Have answered me as if they knew my woe,
And it might seem have fashioned so their rime
To be my own soul's cry; easing the flow
Of my dumb tears with language sweet as sobs,
Yet are there days when all these hoards of thought
Hold nothing for me. Not one verse that throbs
Throbs with my head, or as my brain is fraught.

'Tis then I voice mine own weird reveries:
Low croonings of a motherless child, in gloom
Singing his frightened self to sleep, are these.
One night, if thou shouldst lie in this Sick Room
Dreading the Dark thou darest not illume;
Listen; my voice may haply lend thee ease.

Antaeus: A Fragment

So neck to stubborn neck, and obstinate knee to knee,
Wrestled those two; and peerless Heracles
Could not prevail, nor get at any vantage
So those huge hands that, small, had snapped great snakes,
Let slip the writhing of Antaeus' wrists:
Those hero's hands that wrenched the necks of bulls,
Now fumbled round the slim Antaeus' limbs,
Baffled. Then anger swelled in Heracles,
And terribly he grappled broader arms,
And yet more firmly fixed his grasped feet.
And up his back the muscles bulged and shone
Like climbing banks and domes of towering cloud.
And they who watched that wrestling say he laughed,
But not so loud as on Eurystheus of old.

The Promisers

When I awoke, the glancing day looked gay;
The air said: Fare you fleetly; you will meet him!
And when the prosp'rous sun was well begun,
I heard a bird say: Sweetly you shall greet him!

The sun fell strong and bold upon my shoulder;
It hung, it clung as it were my friend's arm.
The birds fifed on before, shrill-piping pipers,
Right down to town; and there they ceased to charm.

And there I wandered till the noon came soon,
And chimed: The time is hastening with his face!
Sly twilight said: I bring him; wait till late!
But darkness harked forlorn to my lone pace.

The Fates

They watch me, those informers to the Fates,
Called Fortune, Chance, Necessity, and Death;
Time, in disguise as one who serves and waits,
Eternity, as girls of fragrant breath.
I know them. Men and Boys are in their pay,
And those I hold my trustiest friends may prove
Agents of Theirs to take me if I stray
From fatal ordinance. If I move they move,—

Escape? There is one unwatched way: your eyes,
O Beauty! Keep me good that secret gate!
And when the cordon tightens of the spies
Let the close iris of your eyes grow great.
So I'll evade the vice and rack of age
And miss the march of lifetime, stage by stage.

This is the Track

This is the track my life is setting on,
    Spacious the spanless way I wend;
The blackness of darkness may be held for me?
    And barren plunging without end?

Why dare I fear? For other wandering souls
    Burn thro' the night of that far bourne.
And they are light unto themselves; and aureoles
    Self-radiated there are worn.

And when in after-times we make return
    Round solar bounds awhile to run,
They gather many satellites astern
    And turn aside the very sun.

O World of many Worlds

O World of many Worlds; O life of lives,
  What centre hast thou? Where am I?
O whither is it thy fierce onrush drives?
  Fight I, or drift; or stand or fly?

The loud machinery spins, thy work in touch;
  Wheels whirl in systems, zone in zone.
I myself, having sometime moved with such,
  Would strike a centre of mine own.

Lend hand, O Fate, for I am down, am lost!
  Fainting by violence of the Dance . . .
Ah thanks, I stand—the floor is crossed,
  And I am where but few advance.

I see men far below me where they swarm . . .
  Haply above me—be it so!
Does space to compass-points confirm,
  And can we say a star stands high or low?

Not more complex the millions of the stars
  Than are the hearts of mortal brothers;
As far remote as Neptune from small Mars
  Is one man's nature from another's.

But all hold course unalterably fixed;
  They follow destinies foreplanned:
I envy not these lives their faith unmixed,
  I would not step with such a band.

To be a meteor, fast, eccentric, lone,
  Lawless; in passage through all spheres,
Warning the earth of wider ways unknown
  And rousing men with heavenly fears—

This is the track reserved for my endeavour;
  Spanless the erring way I wend.
Blackness of darkness is my meed for ever?
  And barren plunging without end?

O glorious fear! Those other wandering souls
     High burning through that outer bourne
Are lights unto themselves. Fair aureoles
     Self-radiated there are worn.

And when in after times those stars return
     And strike once more earth's horizon,
They gather many satellites astern,
       For they are greater than this system's sun.

Song of Songs

Sing me at morn but only with your laugh;
Even as Spring that laugheth into leaf;
Even as Love that laugheth after Life.

Sing me but only with your speech all day,
As voluble leaflets do; let viols die;
The least word of your lips is melody!

Sing me at eve but only with your sigh!
Like lifting seas it solaceth; breathe so,
Slowly and low, the sense that no songs say.

Sing me at midnight with your murmurous heart!
Let youth's immortal-moaning chords be heard
Throbbing through you, and sobbing, unsubdued.

All Sounds have been as Music

All sounds have been as music to my listening:
    Pacific lamentations of slow bells,
The crunch of boots on blue snow rosy-glistening,
    Shuffle of autumn leaves; and all farewells:

Bugles that sadden all the evening air,
    And country bells clamouring their last appeals
Before the music of the evening prayer;
    Bridges, sonorous under carriage wheels.

Gurgle of sluicing surge through hollow rocks,
    The gluttonous lapping of the waves on weeds,
Whisper of grass; the myriad-tinkling flocks,
    The warbling drawl of flutes and shepherds' reeds.

The orchestral noises of October nights
    Blowing [   ] symphonetic storms
Of startled clarions [   ]
    Drums, rumbling and rolling thunderous and [   ]

Thrilling of throstles in the keen blue dawn,
    Bees fumbling and fuming over sainfoin-fields.

Bugles Sang

Bugles sang, saddening the evening air,
And bugles answered, sorrowful to hear.

Voices of boys were by the river-side.
Sleep mothered them; and left the twilight sad.
The shadow of the morrow weighed on men.

Voices of old despondency resigned,
Bowed by the shadow of the morrow, slept.

[   ] dying tone
Of receding voices that will not return.
The wailing of the high far-travelling shells
And the deep cursing of the provoking [   ].

The monstrous anger of our taciturn guns.
The majesty of the insults of their mouths.

1914

War broke: and now the Winter of the world
With perishing great darkness closes in.
The foul tornado, centred at Berlin,
Is over all the width of Europe whirled,
Rending the sails of progress. Rent or furled
Are all Art's ensigns. Verse wails. Now begin
Famines of thought and feeling. Love's wine's thin.
The grain of human Autumn rots, down-hurled.

For after Spring had bloomed in early Greece,
And Summer blazed her glory out with Rome,
An Autumn softly fell, a harvest home,
A slow grand age, and rich with all increase.
But now, for us, wild Winter, and the need
Of sowings for new Spring, and blood for seed.

The One Remains

I sometimes think of those pale, perfect faces
My wonder has not looked upon, as yet;
And of those others never to be met;
And often pore I on the secret traces
Left in my heart, of countenances seen,
And lost as soon as seen,—but which mine eye
Remembers as my old home, or the lie
Of landscapes whereupon my windows lean.

And as for those long known and worshipped long,
But now, alas! no longer, and the song
Of voices that have said 'Adieu, we part,'
Their reminiscences would cease my heart,
Except I still hoped find, some time, some place,
All beauty, once for ever, in one face.

To the Bitter Sweet-heart: a Dream

One evening Eros took me by the hand,
    And having folded feathers round my head,
Or sleep like feathers, towards a far hope sped,
    I groping, for he bade me understand
He would soon fill with Your's my other hand.
But when I heard his singing wings expand
    My face fell deeply in his shoulder.
    Sweet moons we flew thus, yet I waned not older
But in his exquisiteness I flagged, unmanned
Till, when his wings were drooping to an end,
Feeling my empty hand fulfilled with His,
I knew Love gave himself my passion-friend.
So my old quest of you requited is,
Ampler than e'er I asked of your girl's grace.
I shall not ask you more, nor see your face.

The Sleeping Beauty

Sojourning through a southern realm in youth,
I came upon a house by happy chance
Where bode a marvellous Beauty. There, romance
Flew faerily until I lit on truth—
For lo! the fair Child slumbered. Though, forsooth,
She lay not blanketed in drowsy trance,
But leapt alert of limb and keen of glance,
From sun to shower; from gaiety to ruth;
Yet breathed her loveliness asleep in her:
For, when I kissed, her eyelids knew no stir.
So back I drew tiptoe from that Princess,
Because it was too soon, and not my part,
To start voluptuous pulses in her heart,
And kiss her to the world of Consciousness.

Sonnet Autumnal

If it be very strange and sorrowful
To scent the first night-frost in autumntide:
If on the sombre day when Summer died
Men shuddered, awed to hear her burial:
And if the dissolution of one rose
(Whereof the future holds unnumbered store)
Engender human tears,—ah! how much more
Sorrows and suffers he whose sense foreknows
The weakening and the withering of a love,
The dying of a love that had been dear!
Who feels upon a hand, but late love-warm,
A hardness of indifference, like a glove;
And in the dead calm of a voice may hear
The menace of a drear and mighty storm.

Long Ages Past

Long ages past in Egypt thou wert worshipped
And thou wert wrought from ivory and beryl.
They brought thee jewels and they brought their slain,
Thy feet were dark with blood of sacrifice.
From dawn to midnight, O my painted idol,
Thou satest smiling, and the noise of killing
Was harp and timbrel in thy pale jade ears:
The livid dead were given thee for toys.

*   *   *

Thou wert a mad slave in a Persian palace,
And the King loved thee for thy furious beauty,
And all men heard thy ravings with a smile
Because thy face was fairer than a flower.
But with a little knife so wantonly
Thou slewest women and thy pining lovers,
And on thy lips the stain of crimson blood,
And on thy brow the pallor of their death.

*   *   *

Thou art the dream beheld by frenzied princes
In smoke of opium—thou art the last fulfilment
Of all the wicked, and of all the beautiful.
We hold thee as a poppy to our mouths,
Finding with thee forgetfulness of God.
Thou art the face reflected in a mirror
Of wild desire, of pain, of bitter pleasure.
The witches shout thy name beneath the moon,
The fires of Hell have held thee in their fangs.

Purple

Vividly gloomy, with bright darkling glows
Of fine stars, or night-sparkling southern shores;
Stain of strong fruits, wines, passions, and the cores
Of all quick hearts! Yet from its deepness blows
Aroma and romance of violets;
Softness of far land, lost; pacific lift
Of smoke through quiet trees; and that wild drift
Of smoulder where the flame of evening sets.
Yea, that columnar, thunder-throning cloud
Wears it so stately that therein the King
Stands before men, and lies in death's hands, proud.
Purest, it is a diamond dawn of Spring,
And yet the Veil of Venus and youth's skin
Mauve-marbled; purpling young Love's mouth for sacred sin.

Maundy Thursday

Between the brown hands of a server-lad
The silver cross was offered to be kissed.
The men came up, lugubrious, but not sad,
And knelt reluctantly, half-prejudiced.
(And kissing, kissed the emblem of a creed.)
Then mourning women knelt; meek mouths they had,
(And kissed the Body of the Christ indeed.)
Young children came, with eager lips and glad.
(These kissed a silver doll, immensely bright.)
Then I, too, knelt before that acolyte.
Above the crucifix I bent my head:
The Christ was thin, and cold, and very dead:
And yet I bowed, yea, kissed—my lips did cling
(I kissed the warm live hand that held the thing.)

To—

Three rompers run together, hand in hand.
The middle boy stops short, the others hurtle:
What bumps, what shrieks, what laughter turning turtle.
Love, racing between us two, has planned
A sudden mischief: shortly he will stand
And we shall shock. We cannot help but fall;
What matter? Why, it will not hurt at all,
Our youth is supple, and the world is sand.

Better our lips should bruise our eyes, than He,
Rude love, out-run our breath; you pant, and I,
I cannot run much farther; mind that we
Both laugh with love; and having tumbled, try
To go forever children, hand in hand.
The sea is rising . . . and the world is sand.

May 10, 1916.
London.

Spells and Incantation (a Fragment)

A vague pearl, a wan pearl
You showed me once: I peered through far-gone winters
Until my mind was fog-bound in that gem.

Blue diamonds, cold diamonds
You shook before me, so that out of them
Glittered and glowed vast diamond dawns of spring.

Tiger-eyed rubies, wrathful rubies
You rolled. I watched their hot hearts fling
Flames from each glaring summer of my life.

Quiet amber, mellow amber
You lifted; and behold the whole air rife
With evening, and the auburn autumn cloud. . . .

The Imbecile

The imbecile with long light hair, so light
That in the moon it shineth white;
The imbecile with fair long hair, so long
It falleth all her length along,
     She nothing knoweth of her wrong.

The imbecile with large green eyes, so clear
Therein her strange soul's deeps appear;
The imbecile with large clear eyes, so green
You see her very dreams between,
     Foldeth her angel hands serene.

Beauty

The beautiful, the fair, the elegant,
Is that which pleases us, says Kant,
Without a thought of interest or advantage.

I used to watch men when they spoke of beauty
And measure their enthusiasm. One,
An old man, seeing a [   ] setting sun
Praised it [[a certain sense of duty
To the calm evening and his time of life.
I know another man that never says a Beauty
But of a horse;

*　　*　　*

Men seldom speak of beauty, beauty as such,
Not even lovers think about it much.
Women of course consider it for hours
In mirrors;

*　　*　　*

A Shrapnel Ball

A shrapnel ball
Just where the wet skin glistened when he swam.
Like a full-opened sea-anemone.
We both said 'What a beauty! What a beauty, lad!'
I knew that in that flower he saw a hope
Of living on, and seeing again tile roses of his home.
Beauty is that which pleases and delights,
Not bringing personal advantage—Kant.
But later on I heard
A canker worked into that crimson flower
And that he sank with it
And laid it with the anemones off Dover.

Bold Horatius

Having, with bold Horatius, stamped her feet
And waved a final swashing arabesque
O'er the brave days of old, she ceased to bleat,
Slapped her Macaulay back upon the desk,
Resumed her calm gaze and her lofty seat.

There, while she heard the classic lines repeat,
Once more the teacher's face clenched stern;
For through the window, looking on the street,
Three soldiers hailed her. She made no return.
One was called 'Orace whom she would not greet.

Elegy in April and September

(jabbered among the trees)

Hush, thrush!
Hush, missen-thrush, I listen . . .
I heard the flush of footsteps through the loose leaves,
And a low whistle by the water's brim.

Be still, daffodil!
And wave me not so bravely.
Your gay gold lily daunts me and deceives,
Who follow gleams more golden and more slim.

Look, brook!
O run and look, O run!
The vain reeds shook . . . Yet search till gray sea heaves,
And I will wind among these fields for him.

Gaze, daisy!
Stare up through haze and glare,
And mark the hazardous stars all dawns and eves,
For my eye withers, and his star wanes dim.

To a Comrade in Flanders

Seeing we never spied frail Fairyland,
Though small we crouched by bluebells, moon by moon,
And are too late for Lethe's tide; too soon
For that new bridge that leaves old Styx half-spanned:
Nor meekly unto Mecca caravanned;
Nor bugled Asgard, skilled in magic rune;
Nor yearned for far Nirvana, the sweet swoon;
And are from Paradise cursed out and banned:

Let's die back to those hearths we died for. Thus
Shall we be gods there. Death shall be no sev'rance.
In dull, dim chancels, flower new shrines for us.
For us, rough knees of boys shall ache with rev'rance;
For girls' breasts are the clear white Acropole
Where our own mothers' tears shall heal us whole.

Sept. 1916.

THE BLACKTHORN PRESS

The Blackthorn Press publishes a wide variety of books about local history, English Literature and the arts. Most of our books are available for your Kindle. Visit our website

www.blackthornpress.com

for the latest news and prices.